Dick & Val

# WHO GO



Malcolm

## An Autobiography

**Malcolm Sutherland**

Printed & Published by
Leiston Press Ltd
2014
Unit 1b Masterlord Industrial Estate,
Leiston, Suffolk, IP16 4JD
Tel: 01728 833003
Email: glenn@leistonpress.com
www.leistonpress.com



ISBN: 978-1-907938-78-8

**WHO GOES THERE**

CONTENTS

# INTRODUCTION

The truth, the whole truth and nothing but the truth is a lofty ideal, but no easy task. I shall endeavour to tell the truth, ungarnished – warts and all. I am aware of several pitfalls. First, as Freud has made quite clear, we all have a tendency to repress unsavoury incidents in our lives. Secondly, we all tend to embellish the facts; perhaps to show ourselves in a better light, perhaps to make the story more interesting or more amusing. Thirdly, constant repetition of an inaccuracy leads us to believe that the truth has been established. Fourthly, memories tend to be selective: if we are of a happy disposition, we will tend to remember best the happy incidents in our lives and perhaps gloss over or ignore less happy episodes; alternatively, if we are morose, we may emphasise the tragedies and down-play the strokes of good fortune.

Let me give a few examples of what I mean. A South African friend, who was a company director, said that there was no racial discrimination in his company. All the directors and managers where whites; all the sales representatives were Indians, and all the drivers were blacks. There was no racial discrimination. Ha-ha! But I have failed to say that my friend said that all appointments were strictly on merit and for that reason only "all the directors and managers were whites", and so on. The omission of mentioning merit makes for a more amusing anecdote, but it is a distortion.

Here is another example of a pitfall. When my sister and I were quite young, my father decided that we should learn how to swim. We were given lessons at the White Rock Swimming Baths in Hastings. We had to gird ourselves with webbing belts on the back of which were large metal triangular hooks. We then had to try to swim across the corner of the deep end of the pool. Of course, panic set in and we floundered and started to sink. The instructor then tried to rescue us by inserting a boathook into the metal triangle on the belt and thereby drawing us back to the edge of the pool. Unfortunately, the instructor was unaware of the effects of refraction when a rod is inserted into water. So, instead of connecting hook to triangle, we were poked higher in the back than was necessary and we were pushed down even further into the water. It was disastrous, but that is not the point of the story. The experience was firmly etched on both my and my sister's minds. My sister was convinced that the instructor was a man: I was equally convinced that the instructor was a woman. It matters not which of us was right: the point to be made is that in retelling or reliving the incident time and time again, one of us had turned fact into fiction.

Memory, of course, is fickle and becomes more blurred as the years pass. I have never kept a diary. Thus what I record here about myself is certainly not "the whole truth". There are bound to be omissions. But what I have written about myself is as truthful as I can make it and is not embellished.

On a number of occasions, I have used fictitious initials, or a nickname, in the narrative, so as to disguise the names of people who might still be living and who might be embarrassed by what I write about them.

Chapter 1

# WHAT'S IN A NAME? (1) MY FATHER

My father was known to most people as Tommy – not because his name was Thomas, nor because he was a soldier. I believe it was a nickname he acquired when he was at Bedford School, due to the fact that he had rather a rosy complexion (like a tomato). Many years after my father's death, I met a first cousin Jean, whose mother was one of my father's sisters. Jean had no recollection of the Sutherland family calling my father Tommy. They called him by his first name Claud.

To me, Claud is rather an effeminate name - "after you Cecil; no after you Claud", as the saying goes. So I prefer to think of my father as Tommy. In fact, his full name was Claud Ian Sutherland. He repeated the name Ian in the names of both his sons, but when I came to trace Tommy's family tree, there was no earlier Ian. I fancy Tommy was given the initials C.I. to mirror those of his mother, Cordelia Isabel. I still have a table-napkin ring with the entwined initials C.I.S. engraved on it. Did it commemorate my father or my grandmother? There is no way of knowing.

I knew that Tommy was born in Calcutta (on 5 March 1899), that he was the fourth and youngest child of a second marriage of my grandfather, James and that he was orphaned at an early age. I will return to that later. I knew, too, that my grandfather James had been a merchant in Calcutta and that Tommy had had Sutherland cousins with distinguished careers in the Indian Army. Not until many years after Tommy's death, did I become interested in my Sutherland ancestry. It was then too late to quiz him. But by diligent research, I was able to find out a lot more about the Sutherland family in India. I shall also return to that later.

Tommy went from Bedford School to Sandhurst. He was commissioned as an officer into the Argyll and Sutherland

Highlanders shortly before the end of World War I. At Sandhurst, he had distinguished himself as a horseman. He was the runner up for "the saddle" which was awarded to the man adjudged to be the best horseman of the year.

After being commissioned, Tommy was soon posted to the Western Front in France. The casualty rate amongst young British officers was extremely high, but fortunately Tommy survived without injury. He was awarded the Military Cross. The citation reads "on 30 September 1918, east of Pontruet, 2$^{nd}$ Lieutenant Claud Ian Sutherland did splendid work and ably led his platoon, which was first to reach the final objective, in spite of heavy machine-gun fire. His contempt of danger inspired the greatest confidence in his men. On reaching the final objective, he ably assisted the advance of the other platoons by bringing fire to bear on the enemy, who were still holding out on his flanks." Tommy declined to attend an investiture at Buckingham Palace for the Cross to be pinned to his breast by King George V. He was always a bit of a rebel. Was it because he was orphaned at an early age and lacked parental control?

Tommy remained in the army for several years after the Armistice on 11 November 1918 (he was a regular), and saw service in Ireland and in Russia. But I suspect he found army life rather dull and unrewarding after his meteoric rise to Captain during the war. As a peace-time soldier, it would have been many years before he became a substantive Captain, and yet many more before his Majority, in all probability. Whatever his reason, Tommy accepted an offer of redundancy in 1922. After that, he never settled down in a civilian job or profession. At one time or another, he was the factor for Lord Somerleyton, the part owner of a Lowestoft trawler, a trainer of gun dogs and a film director. He called his studios in Wardour Street "Malcolm Studios", after me, and their emblem was a sprig of heather, after my sister Heather. All these ventures ended in failure, and sometimes in bankruptcy.

One consequence was that, after the first few years of marriage, Tommy was unable to support his family. He and my mother lived apart, although they never divorced. My own earliest childhood memories are of the home provided for my mother and her children by *her* mother "Lalla". I had no emotional attachment to my father. Later, it became my responsibility to support my mother. I fear I lost respect for Tommy.

On one memorable occasion, Tommy entertained my mother, my sister Heather and me to lunch at the *Trocadero* in London. It was at the time he had his film studios in Wardour Street. Heather and I were allowed to choose just what we wanted to eat. Heather, 15 months my senior, and a great deal more sophisticated than me, chose chicken – quite a delicacy in the 1930s. I chose sausages and bubble-and-squeak! I duly got them. When the lunch was over, Heather and I were given small presents. My present was a box of chocolate soldiers. My mother was given a white carnation. I asked the waiter "where is Daddy's present"? Tommy quickly interposed "I simply get the bill and pay for the lot"! After lunch, we walked to his Wardour Street office. I was puzzled to see a pair of lady's high-heel shoes under a chair. There was probably an innocent explanation. I didn't ask for one. As far as I know, Tommy had no extra-marital affairs. When I was several years older, I wrote to Tommy reminding him of the vows he took in the church service of Holy Matrimony. I got no reply. I should have received a flea in the ear for being such a prig!

Immediately after the outbreak of World War II, Tommy rejoined his regiment. He had been on the Regular Army Reserve of Officers. He saw service in the western desert, but he never rose above his earlier rank of Captain. My mother had to engage solicitors to compel Tommy to remit to her the marriage allowance to which he was entitled.

Tommy drifted again after leaving the army for the second time when World War II was over. Eventually and tragically he took his own life in 1951. He was only 52 years old. Tommy's was a sad life, not only for him, but also for his wife, and to a much lesser extent for his children, my sister and me.

As I have already mentioned, Tommy was orphaned

when he was quite young. His mother (Cordelia) died from consumption in 1905. Tommy had just turned 6. His father, James, then aged 66, sent Tommy and his three older sisters (all the issue of James's second marriage to Cordelia) to Bedford, England, to be in the care of their aunt (Cordelia's sister) Mrs Clifford. It was an unhappy arrangement. None of the children liked their aunt, and their aunt possibly looked upon them as a tiresome burden.

Tommy's best friend at Bedford School was Guy McJannet. Guy introduced his friend Tommy to his (Guy's) mother and siblings, who were also living in Bedford. Tommy virtually became an additional member of the McJannet household. Guy, who became an officer in the Bedfordshire Regiment, died in August 1918 as a result of a fractured spine caused by gunshot, whilst in action on the Western Front. Five years later, Tommy married Guy's sister – my mother. In later life, I wondered whether Tommy and Guy had a homosexual relationship. Perhaps my mother "caught" Tommy on the rebound, after Guy's tragic death. My mother was eight years Tommy's senior, so another possible explanation of their marriage is that, subconsciously, Tommy was looking for a mother substitute.

Tommy and my mother had three children: Nigel Ian (who survived only one day after a forceps delivery), my sister Heather Mary and me, Malcolm Ian Douglas. I was named Ian after Tommy (really Claud Ian) and Douglas after my godfather, Douglas Fraser McJannet, who was the youngest child in the McJannet household, the brother of my mother and of Guy.

Tommy was an obscure and rather esoteric figure in my childhood. He adored fast cars and several times raced at Brooklands. He was a keen fisherman and a great lover of horses and dogs. As children, my sister and I saw very little of him. I can remember a few visits to the McJannet home which, by that time was also the home of my mother, my sister and me. Once he gave us a spaniel which we called Nelson, because it was blind in one eye. Several years later, when I was at my public school, I recall a visit from my father – possibly on the eve of his embarkation for Egypt and the war in North Africa.

A contemporary of Tommy in the Argyll and Sutherland Highlanders in World War I was G.H.A. Macmillan (nicknamed "the babe"). At the end of World War II, Macmillan was the General Officer Commanding, Palestine. I was a staff officer in Jerusalem at that time. Tommy must have written to Macmillan telling him that I, his son was on his staff. I was summonsed to meet Macmillan, but I have no recollection, at all, of our conversation. Was it about Tommy and their friendship in World War I? Was it simply welcoming me to his staff?

Circumstances conspired to veil in mystery Tommy's origins and relations in India. Tommy was only 8 when his father died, so he probably knew little about his own background. And I, of course, got no information on these matters from Tommy. It was not until I was in my 50s that I became curious to know more about Tommy's family. My starting point was the date of Tommy's birth in Calcutta (March 1899). My great good fortune was to find that the British administration in India and its predecessor, the East India Company, were assiduous recorders of life and events in India. All the records that they kept eventually found their way into the India Office Records and Library in London. (These records were later transferred to the British Library, where they are now to be found). Through the records of births, marriages, deaths and Wills, I was able to construct a Sutherland Family tree. To my great surprise, the first record of a Sutherland ancestor in Calcutta was of a James Sutherland who was a Sergeant in the Bengal Artillery in 1783. Sergeant James died in Calcutta on 28 December 1796. He was my great-great-great grandfather. The Sutherland family had been living in Calcutta for four generations by the time of Tommy's birth in 1899. By the 1930s, however, all of them had either died or had left India for good. An abridged Sutherland Family tree which I managed to piece together is given in Table 1.

*

There was a mystery in the Family Tree which eventually was resolved. It will be seen from Table 1 that Tommy's great grandmother, Mary Harriet Sutherland married another Sutherland – Charles Jackson Sutherland. It is Mary Harriet Sutherland's pedigree which goes back to the James Sutherland who was a Sergeant in the Bengal Artillery. What about Charles Jackson Sutherland's ancestry? Were Charles Jackson and Mary Harriet cousins?

From the details recorded at his death, it is known that Charles Jackson Sutherland was born on 8 August 1810. But I have found no birth registration which would confirm this. And the certificates of his two marriages do not give the correct name of his father. When he married Mary Harriet Sutherland on 21 January 1835, he is described simply as a bachelor, of age. At his second marriage, he was described as a widower *son of Patrick.* But that was surely an error. He was the *son-in-law* of Patrick (Mary Harriet's father). This is confirmed in Patrick's Will. Twice Patrick refers to Charles Jackson as his *son-in-law.*

Since I seemed to be at a dead end, I thought I would try to find other living descendants of Charles Jackson Sutherland and ask them if they had any information about his origins. To my delight, I found I had at least six second cousins, all living in England, none of whom I had met before. One of these cousins was named after Charles Jackson Sutherland. He was baptised Charles Robert Sutherland Graham. Bob Graham was of the opinion that Charles Jackson was born **Brownrigg** and that he had been adopted by Patrick Sutherland (whose daughter, Mary Harriet Sutherland, he later married). Another newly discovered cousin had a piece of jewelry bearing the Brownrigg family crest. Both these facts pointed to the likelihood that my great grandfather was born Charles Jackson **Brownrigg.**

There were several Brownriggs living in India in 1810, but eventually I came to the conclusion that the Brownrigg who fathered Charles Jackson was John Studholme Brownrigg. John Studholme Brownrigg was the Secretary of the Military Board in Calcutta: Patrick Sutherland was the Board's Registrar. Not only were Brownrigg and Sutherland office colleagues, they were also probably friends because a *J.S. Brownrigg* signed as a witness at the Calcutta wedding of a daughter of Patrick, by his first wife.

There is another connection between John Studholme Brownrigg and Charles Jackson Sutherland which seemed to be significant. Brownrigg left the service of the East India Company in 1820 and became a merchant, first in Calcutta and then in London. Later he became the M.P. for Boston in Lincolnshire. In London, Brownrigg was a partner in the firm of *Sir Charles Cockerell & Co.* Robert Howe Cockerell was the senior partner in the Calcutta branch of this company. He was a witness to the wedding of Charles Jackson Sutherland to Mary Harriet Sutherland.

Even more significantly, the first recorded evidence of Charles Jackson Sutherland's employment in Calcutta was in the Calcutta branch of *Cockerell & Company.*

John Studholme Brownrigg married in Calcutta in December 1812, two years after the birth of Charles Jackson. He was then described as a bachelor. If, therefore, he was Charles Jackson's father, it would seem that he did not marry Charles Jackson's mother. My theory is that Charles Jackson's mother died when her child was an infant and Brownrigg then arranged for his married friend and colleague, Patrick Sutherland, to adopt and bring up the infant boy as his own. The episode would have been hushed up, in view of Brownrigg's wedding and later distinguished career. Then, my theory went, Brownrigg secured a good post in Calcutta for his illegitimate son, once he had reached manhood.

John Studholme Brownrigg came from a more distinguished family than the Sutherland family in India. I had hoped that the extant legitimate descendant of Brownrigg, namely Henry John Studholme Brownrigg, might have documentation in support of my theory, But I have failed to get a response from him. However, I have become a friend of another Henry Brownrigg, who happily refers to me as *Cousin Malcolm*!

This Henry Brownrigg and I underwent DNA testing. It

showed that there was a 98% probability that we had a common ancestor. My conclusion is that Charles Jackson Sutherland was almost certainly the son of John Studholme Brownrigg.

*

It may be of interest to record that one of Tommy's uncles, Arthur Benoni Sutherland married a girl called Louisa Fanny Orr. Her father was Captain Patrick Orr, who was killed in the Indian Mutiny of 1857. That branch of the Sutherland family has adopted the middle name of *Orr.* It was principally Orr Sutherland cousins whom I met in England. Since I have no family myself, I have handed over my Sutherland family papers to Charles Arthur Orr Sutherland.

*

I should dearly love to know the origins of my ancestor James Sutherland, who was the Sergeant in the Bengal Artillery in the 1780s. My strong suspicion is that James was a soldier in Macleod's Highlanders or the Seaforth Highlanders or the Royal Highland Regiment, British regiments of Scots who were serving in India in the late 18th century, and that he left his regiment for a more lucrative appointment in the Bengal Artillery. I do not think that James was recruited by the East India Company in Britain. There are reasonable records of these appointments. James's name does not figure in them. It will be seen from Table 1 that James's son Patrick married, secondly Sarah Eleanor Byrn. She was the daughter of Sergeant Wale Byrn (1763-1801) whose appointment in the Bengal Army is clearly recorded. He was recruited by the East India Company in 1778.

James's wife, Ann may well have been an Indian or Anglo-Indian. It is known that, even in 1810 – many years after James's marriage – there were only an estimated 250 white women in Bengal, among upwards of 2,000 white men. Similarly, Charles Jackson Sutherland's mother may well have been of Indian descent.

*

Tommy said that his ancestors came from Lairg, in the county of Sutherland, but there is no proof of this. Tommy also claimed that the Sutherlands in India had Chinese blood. I believe it far more likely that they had Indian blood. Christopher Hawes in his book about Anglo-Indians, entitled *Poor Relations*, asserts quite categorically that Patrick Sutherland was Anglo-Indian. Certainly, his post as Registrar of the Military Board in Calcutta lends credence to this statement. Furthermore, photographs of Charles Jackson Sutherland and of Arthur Benoni Sutherland and his family are strongly suggestive of Indian blood,

On the other hand, it has to be said that it was most unusual for a man of mixed blood to be appointed as an underwriter in the Indian Civil Service (I.C.S.), considered - by themselves – to be *God's Elect*! Yet Patrick Sutherland's youngest son, Henry Cobbe Sutherland (1834-1878) became an underwriter in the I.C.S. (In contrast, many officers in the Indian Army were of mixed blood).

*

The Sutherland family lived in Calcutta for some 150 years (five generations) from the 1780s to thc 1930s. Unlikc most British residents in Bengal who sent their children home to be educated and who themselves left India when they retired, the Sutherlands made Bengal their home for at least 100 years. Only towards the end of the period of 150 years were Sutherland children sent to England to be educated and Sutherland men left India when they retired. This phenomenon lends credence to the theory, commented on previously, that Indian as well as Scots blood flowed in the veins of the Sutherlands in India.

*

In the 1780s, subsequent to the battles of Plassey (1757) and Buxar (1766), the British East India Company was firmly in control of Bengal and its capital city of Calcutta. The Company had found it necessary to defend its lucrative trading operations by establishing its own armed forces not only in Bengal, but also in Bombay and Madras. It was in the Company's Bengal army that Sergeant James Sutherland ended his short military career. He was too young to have seen action at Plassey or Buxar and there is no record of the Bengal Artillery, in which James served, being in action during his years of service with them.

Sergeant James married in Calcutta and had a son, Patrick, born there in 1784. Patrick had a quasi-military career in that he became the Registrar of the Military Board in Calcutta. Patrick married in Calcutta, a girl born in Calcutta, and all their children were born in Calcutta. Their youngest son, however, went to Oxford University and, as already mentioned, had a career in the Indian Civil Service. Patrick's eldest daughter, Mary Harriet Sutherland and her husband Charles Jackson Sutherland (presumed born in Calcutta) had a large family, all born and educated in Calcutta. Many of their grandchildren, however, were educated in England. Although some of them returned to India to serve in the Indian Army, they all retired to England. By the late 19$^{th}$ century some Sutherlands were wealthy merchants, financially able to educate their sons outside India and perhaps to buy them army commissions.

In 1857, soldiers in the Bengal army mutinied – some call this mutiny the First Indian War of Independence. As already noted, a Sutherland married an Orr whose father was slaughtered in the mutiny, The mutiny was put down, brutally in many instances, but the East India Company was obliged to cede its power to the British government and the three East India Company's regiments were brought under the control of the British army. Did the Sutherlands see the writing on the wall – an eventual independent India and the loss of British suzerainty? The road to independence was lengthy, but shortly after World War II India was partitioned and became two independent countries. By that time the Sutherland presence in Bengal was extinct.

*

I shall now turn to my mother's family the *McJannets.*

## TABLE 1: SUTHERLAND FAMILY TREE

James Sutherland = Ann
1757-1796

Wale Byrn = Mary Christian
1763-1808

Patrick Sutherland = (1) Anne Balfour
1784-1856 1787-1815

= (2) Sarah Eleanor Byrn
1793-1855

Mary Harriet Sutherland = Charles Jackson Sutherland
1816-1846 1810-1897

James Sutherland = (1) Louisa Esther Collins (nee Brann) = (2) Cordelia Isabella Batho
1839-1907 1871-1905

Claud Ian (Tommy) Sutherland = Janet Mary (Jean) McJannet
1899-1951 1893-1979

The Author

---

## TABLE 2: BROWNRIGG DESCENT

|

Henry Brownrigg (of Wingfield) d.1723 m. Joan Symes

|

John Brownrigg (of Tubberpatrick) m. Mary Studholme

|

Henry Brownrigg (of Rockingham) d.1793 m. Mary Alcock

|

John Studholme Brownrigg d.1787 m. Lydia Eames

|

John Studholme Brownrigg 1786-1853

|

Charles Jackson Sutherland 1810-1897

|

(See Table 1)

## TABLE 3: McJANNET DESCENT

William McJannet (in Dunree)

|

Alexander McJannet (in Dunree) b.1697 m.1732 Mary Dunlop

|

Alexander William McJannet (in Maybole) b.1732 m. Agnes Watt

|

William McJannet (farmer in East Brocklock) 1759-1842 m.1782 Margaret Bryan

|

Thomas McJannet (land steward) 1792-1854 m.1819 Jean (or Jane) Baines

|

John McJannet (draper) 1823-1875 m.1850 Elizabeth Eliza Beckett

|

James McJannet (pharmacist) 1851-1939 m.1881 Mary Ann Sophia Morris

|

Janet Mary(Jean) McJannet 1893-1979 m.1923 Claud Ian Sutherland

|

The Author

1. Mary Harriet Sutherland
( Great Grandmother)

2. James Sutherland
(Grandfather)

3. Cordelia Sutherland
(née Batho) (Grandmother)

4. Cordelia Sutherland with my
Father

5. Sutherland Siblings, my Father, May, Enid and Eileen (c.1902)

6. Aunts Enid & Eileen Sutherland

7. C.I. (Tommy) Sutherland (my Father) (c.1918)

8. The Orr Sutherlands – Arthur Benoni and Louisa Fanny Sutherland & Family

9. Sutherland Cousins – Charles Sutherland, Author, Robert Sutherland (Son of Charles),
Hazel Heywood (Granddaughter of Arthur Benoni Sutherland),
Isabel King (née Sutherland),
Emma Sutherland (Daughter of Charles),
Irene Campbell (Granddaughter of Arthur Benoni Sutherland),
Daugher of Isobel King

10. Heather Mary Brownstein (née Sutherland) (Sister)

Chapter 2

# WHAT'S IN A NAME? (2) MY MOTHER

## McJannet

My mother was known to most people as Jean. Tommy, who had a ready wit, called her High Jean (Hygiene) because she was a scrupulously clean housewife. Tommy once had a secretary called Miss Carter, who suffered from body odour. He called her Pizzicato (Pitsy Carter). It will become clear in later chapters that Jean was central in my life, throughout most of her life.

In fact, Jean was born Janet Mary McJannet. This has a nice ring to it. It gave rise to the myth (held, amongst others, by the history master at Bedford Girls School, where Jean was educated) that a Donald McDonald escaped to France from Glencoe, after the massacre there in 1692, and, fearful that King William's troops would continue to chase him, adopted his wife's first name Janet as a new surname. Thereafter, the eldest daughter was always to be called Janet McJannet. Perhaps my grandfather James McJannet believed this myth. Certainly his eldest daughter, my mother, was baptised Janet McJannet. But when I researched the McJannet family, I discovered that the surname of McJannet preceded the massacre of Glencoe. It is a most uncommon Scottish surname, probably derived from Glen Gennet in Ayrshire. Certainly, it was in Ayrshire that the McJannet family proliferated throughout the years. Jean's father James was born in North Walsham, Norfolk. But his father, John had migrated to Norfolk from Ayrshire.

I have traced James's pedigree to a William McJannet who lived in Dunree, Ayrshire in the late 17th century (see Table 3).

My grandfather James McJannet was educated in the local school at North Walsham (at one time attended by Nelson) and subsequently qualified as a pharmaceutical chemist. After practising for a short time in London, he migrated to South

Africa. There he married (in 1881) a South African born girl (Mary Ann Sophia Morris). James worked first for *Lennon Ltd.* in Port Elizabeth and East London before (in 1879) establishing his own pharmacy in East London, with a branch in Fort Beaufort. James's wife, Mary was known to my sister and me as Lalla.

James and Lalla's eldest son Charles, born when Lalla was not yet 20 years old, blotted his copybook. Some say that he got a girl pregnant before he married her: others say that he forged his father's signature on a cheque. Whatever the reason, Charles was cut off and banished to Australia by my grandfather. It must have been a bitter blow for Lalla who, throughout her life, was very family-oriented.

James was not satisfied with the education available to his three eldest sons in South Africa at that time. He thought his remaining seven children would fare better in life if they had an English education. Lalla, my grandmother, was therefore despatched to England with her seven youngest children, in 1908, with the express purpose of securing an English education for them. The family settled in Bedford, where all the children went to school. Jean (my mother) was the eldest of the seven children who left South Africa. She was aged 15 in 1908 and had to help Lalla both on the sea voyage and later in England itself. She became devoted to the youngest sibling (aged 4 in 1908) Douglas Fraser McJannet. Douglas later became my godfather and helped in paying my school fees.

James McJannet's business prospered in East London. He had a lucrative contract to supply the British army with medical supplies during the Anglo-Boer War of 1899-1902. He arranged for his sister Annie (Anna Sophia) to come out to South Africa to nurse wounded soldiers. Annie returned to Norfolk after the war and died there, a spinster, in 1947. After 1908, James made periodic trips to England to see his wife and family. He finally retired to England in the 1930s. The business was then taken over by his son Herbert James McJannet (my Uncle Bertie). Bertie had also qualified in England as a pharmacist.

James, my McJannet grandfather, died in Hastings in

June 1939. I remember him well in his old age – always very properly dressed, with a stiff collar; always taking a cold bath in the morning, whatever the weather, but indulgent to his two grandchildren, Heather and me. After Sunday lunch, the adults would go into the drawing room for a post-prandial snooze, whilst Heather and I had to remain sitting quietly in the dining room. We were enjoined not to disturb the grown-ups. I remember that, on at least one occasion, my grandfather slipping out of the drawing room, returning to the dining room, sitting Heather on the dining room table and giving the table a finishing gloss by pushing her up, down and around, in her knickers. It was difficult to maintain our silence!

At Easter one year, Heather and I had bought a chocolate fish to give to our grandfather. Jean (my mother) told us to write on the greetings card *a sprat to catch a mackerel.* I had no idea what this meant, but Jean knew that our grandfather had bought each of us a wristwatch for Easter – our very first watches.

I have already mentioned Uncles Charles (sent to Australia) and my Uncle Bertie (who took over the pharmaceutical business in East London). Bertie became the Mayor of East London. I shall now pen a few words about Jean's other siblings, in order of their seniority.

Francis Vincent (Uncle Frank) was James's second son. He joined the Merchant Navy. He lost his life in July 1914, as a result of ptomaine poisoning. At least, he escaped a hazardous life at sea during World War I.

Arthur William (Uncle Arthur) was James's fourth son. He gained an agricultural qualification, but his career had hardly got going before World War I started. Uncle Arthur enlisted in South Africa, came to England and was commissioned into the Royal Flying Corps. He lost his life in action in December 1917.

Henry Gordon (Uncle Gordon) was James's fifth son. He was a wizard at figures, although he never qualified as a Chartered Accountant. He was too young to fight in World War I. After school at Bedford, he migrated to India. There he married an Anglo-Indian. They had no family. Uncle Gordon died in

East London in September 1947, while he was staying with his brother (Uncle Bertie).

James's second daughter came next. (Jean, it will be remembered was the eldest daughter). This second daughter was baptised Marjorie Isabel, but she was universally known as *Beaunes*. This nickname originated from her practice of standing beside her father when he was eating chicken, and begging to be given a chicken bone. But Marjorie was sophisticated: *Bones* soon became *Beaunes*. Her fiancé (I doubt whether they were engaged) was a man called Francis (Frank) Bolster, the son of a vicar in Bedford. Sadly, Frank was a World War I casualty. He died in April 1917, aged only 20.

Beaunes, when I knew her, worked for the Savoy Hotel in London. Her task was to find out the likes and dislikes of the hotel's wealthy and prestigious guests, so that on their subsequent visits everything was to their particular liking. Beaunes married Audley Gosling during World War II. They had no children, although both had long lives.

James's next child was another son, Walter Guy (Uncle Guy). It was Guy who was Tommy's great friend at Bedford School and who lost his life in the closing stages of World War I.

Then came James's youngest daughter who was baptised Muriel Frances. Heather and I always called her *Moonie.* She became the secretary of O.P. Beaman, Chairman of the *Orient Shipping Line*. Moonie also married during World War II. Her husband was Harold Mills, youngest son of the food importer A.J. Mills. Harold, at first, was Beaunes's boy-friend. When Moonie rang up Beaunes to say that she was engaged to Harold, Beaunes struck quickly and snapped up Audley Gosling! She then phoned the Social Editor of *The Times* and told him that her own engagement notice should appear before Moonie's engagement notice, since she (Beaunes) was the senior sister! The two engagement notices duly appeared, in that order, in the same issue of *The Times.*

Beaunes and Moonie had a love-hate relationship. Fundamentally, they were very fond of one another, but their relationship was tinged with a streak of jealousy. Moonie, at one time, lent Beaunes a small upholstered armchair. Several years later, she asked for its return. Beaunes refused. Beaunes claimed that the chair was a gift, not a loan. A ding-dong argument ensued in the Grill Room of the Savoy Hotel. Moonie eventually got her chair back: it became known as *the bone of contention.* It became the favourite chair of Harold. It is said, perhaps inaccurately, that he was sitting in it when he died. Harold and Moonie had no children. They were always exceptionally kind to Heather and me.

I have already mentioned James's youngest son, Douglas Fraser (Uncle Douglas). Douglas was perhaps the cleverest of the 10 children. He gained his M.A. at Oriel College, Oxford, returned to the land of his birth and became a preparatory school headmaster in Johannesburg. He was a talented musician (pianist and composer) and a good artist. Three of his oil paintings of South African landscapes and seascapes adorn my drawing room walls.

Douglas himself, when he was a young man, had his portrait painted three times by the distinguished South African artist Hugo Naudé. Douglas had good looks, but one cannot see him being used as a professional model. I wonder whether Naudé was in love with him!

Douglas had a dry sense of humour. Here are two examples. When he was motoring in the Kruger Game Reserve with Jean, the gear lever came loose. Jean (*Hygiene*, you will recall) had a penchant for TCP as a cure-all. Douglas said to Jean "Have you got your bottle of TCP with you? Perhaps that might fix it"!

A second example – although fluent in French himself, Douglas didn't teach French at his school. A mistress taught French. When asked to dinner one evening, Douglas replied "I am sorry, but Wednesdays are the evenings I spend with my French mistress".

Douglas was a popular schoolmaster with the boys. They called him *Jane* (McJannet abbreviated).

*

Douglas was on a motoring holiday in France. When he booked into his hotel he noticed that Mr and Mrs Donald MacJannet had already booked in. With a shared unusual surname (Donald had converted Mc into Mac), Douglas decided to introduce himself to Donald and Charlotte. The two men were not related, but Douglas discovered that he and Donald had something else in common. They were both schoolmasters. Donald (an American) ran a private school near Paris. (Prince Philip, later Duke of Edinburgh, had been a pupil at Donald's school). Douglas and Donald became friends.

Bertie's daughter RuthMary (Douglas's niece) was the victim of a serious road accident in South Africa, with consequent head injuries. Her recovery was slow. Donald and Charlotte (MacJannet) offered her convalescence in France. Thanks to their sympathetic care, RuthMary made a full recovery. The key to her rehabilitation was a cordon bleu cookery course. RuthMary was a beautiful young girl. She received a proposal of marriage from a wealthy French aristocrat, but she turned him down, returned to South Africa and there married Edward Gilfillan, who was the driver of the car in the road accident.

Donald MacJannet was an alumnus of Toft's University. He organised holiday courses for Toft's undergraduates on the shores of Lake Annecy. He and Charlotte retired. They bought an 11th century monastery at Talloires which they set about restoring with the help of Toft's undergraduates. My niece Rosemary helped the MacJannets at *La Prieuré* one summer. My aunt Moonie subscribed to the *MacJannet Foundation.*

After Donald's death, Charlotte moved into a flat in central Geneva. There, RuthMary and I paid her a long visit. We had a day's outing to Talloires, we lunched in the restaurant in the United Nations building in Geneva and RuthMary and I entertained Charlotte to a performance of an oratorio in a Genevan church.

*

Bertie, Moonie and Douglas all died from cancer. So did their mother, Lalla. Beaunes, who was considered to be the most delicate of the McJannet children, outlived all her siblings and was nearly 93 when she died in 1991. Her idiosyncrasies became more and more pronounced with her advancing years. Once I had forcibly to restrain her from stopping the ambulance men from taking her bed-bound husband, Audley to hospital. I held her firmly in my arms. She gave me a good bite! But when Heather and I were children, Beaunes was a never-failing source of fun. She never minded how much we teased her.

*

In South Africa, the McJannets and the Robbs were close family friends. But for the fact that the Robb's only son, Douglas was killed in World War I, he would almost certainly have married Jean (later my mother). Douglas Robb was a 2nd Lieutenant in the South African Infantry. He died in France in March 1918, aged 26.

My grandmother, Jean and later I kept in touch with Douglas's three sisters throughout their lives in South Africa. They all married – Agnes Ball, Pera Holmwood and Mary Wilmot. I was very fond of Pera and always saw her, if I could, when I was in the Cape.

*

My branch of the McJannet family, in stark contrast to my branch of the Sutherland clan, was a bedrock affording me great support over many years. My McJannet grandparents provided a home for my mother, my sister and me, after my mother's marriage floundered. My uncle Douglas McJannet paid for my education at a preparatory school and then at a public school. My uncles Bertie and Douglas McJannet supported and helped my mother and my sister when they emigrated to South Africa immediately after the end of World War II, My aunt Moonie McJannet (Muriel Mills) became a welcoming haven for my mother and me whenever we came to England. She offered financial support if I decided to establish myself as a Land Surveyor in private practice when I was in Africa.

*

I have handed over my McJannet family papers, and those relating to my grandmother (James McJannet's wife) to Uncle Bertie's son, Ian McJannet, in Grahamstown, South Africa. I shall now write a few words about my grandmother.

11. James McJannet
(Grandfather)

12. Mary Ann Sophia McJannet
(née Morris) (Grandmother) 1906

13 Mary McJannet (Lalla)
(Grandmother) 1930s

14. Herbert James McJannet
(Uncle Bertie) (c.1910)

15. Walter Guy McJannet (Uncle Guy, standing with my Father seated)

16. McJannet Siblings: Muriel Mills (Aunt Moonie), Marjorie Gosling (Aunt Beaunes) Douglas Fraser (Uncle Douglas), Janet Mary Sutherland (Mother) (1966)

17. Uncle Douglas – Pencil Sketch by Hugo Naudé

17. McJannet Grandchildren: RuthMary (Gilfillan), Heather Mary (Brownstein), Author, Ian McJannet (2004)

Chapter 3

## WHAT'S IN A NAME? (3) MY GRANDMOTHER

As mentioned previously, Heather and I called my grandmother *Lalla*, a childish corruption of Nana. She became known as Lalla to all the family. In reality, she was born Mary Ann Sophia Morris, in Simon's Town, South Africa. Little is known about her father James Bailey Morris, who was born in Derbyshire in 1836. It is thought that he was a merchant seaman who jumped ship in Simon's Town. There he became a storekeeper and the Junior Warden in a Masonic Lodge. He married Isabella Charlotte Maskew in Cape Town in 1855. They had three sons and three daughters before James's premature death at the age of 37. All three sons and one daughter died in infancy. The surviving children were Lalla and her elder sister Susannah Charlotte Maskew Morris. Aunt Susie, as my mother Jean called her, married Frederick Christian Wienand. They had no son, but I believe there were two daughters. After Lalla's death in 1937, further contact with Aunt Susie and her family evaporated.

Through her mother, Isabella Maskew, Lalla was proud to trace her descent from several of the original Huguenot settlers in the Cape, all of whom arrived between 1686 and 1689. They were: Cecilia D'Atis (d.1739), Marie Buisset (d.c.1751), Jacques De La Porte (d.1739), Pierre Jacobs, Ignace Maré, Marie Menanteau (d.c.1699), Jean Prieur Du Plessis (1638-1708), Hercule Des Pres (d.1695), Anne Retief (d.1710), Pierre Rousseau (d.1719), Susanna Seugnet, Jacques Therod (1668-1739), Francois Du Toit (d.c.1731), Sara Vitout and Suzanne De Vos (d.c.1708).

Jean Prieur Du Plessis was, perhaps, the most illustrious of Lalla'a Huguenot forbears. He was born in Poitiers in 1638 and arrived in the Cape on the *Osterland* in 1688 with his first wife Marie Menanteau and a son. He was a surgeon. He died in Stellenbosch in 1735. Lalla was a descendent of his second son, Jean Louis who was born in Stellenbosch in 1691 and who married Madeleine Rousseau in 1714.

Lalla married James McJannet in Simon's Town, South Africa on 21 September 1881, the day after her 19th birthday. They had ten children, all born in South Africa. As mentioned previously, James was not satisfied with the standard of education received in South Africa by his eldest sons. He therefore sent Lalla off to England in 1908 so that their younger children could get a better education (at Bedford School and Bedford Girls' School). Lalla remained in England for the rest of her life, moving from one rented house to another. She never saw her native South Africa again.

Until her death from cancer in 1935, Lalla was the most important and best loved person in my young life. I loved her even more dearly than my mother and sister. Shortly before her death, I clearly remember Lalla lying ill in bed, on the eve of my departure to my preparatory school. None of us knew how ill she then was. She asked me to sit on the bed by her side and sing to her. (She had a sweet singing voice herself, which my grandfather said should have been trained. There was not much chance for that, if you had 10 children)! I sang to her "I bind unto myself this day, the true name of the Trinity"…. The tears rolled down her cheeks. But her tears were as nothing compared to the ones which I shed myself, when I learnt of her death a few weeks later. My mother Jean had written to my headmaster asking him to break the sad news to me gently. Unfortunately, the headmaster was away when Jean's letter arrived. So when Jean's letter to me (and another from Aunt Moonie) arrived a day or two later, I was completely unprepared. I shut myself up in a lavatory, and shed copious tears. When the headmaster returned, he said "I have heard from your mother that your grandmother has died. Go and sit quietly and write her a letter of condolence, which I want to see in half an hour's time". So much for breaking the news gently!

Lalla was an excellent cook. Sunday lunches were always

a great occasion. (Jean, my sister and I were living with Lalla at this time, and on Sundays we were often joined by one of the aunts, down from London). When lunch was being prepared, I would sit in the kitchen, chatting and hoping for a titbit. Perhaps to stop my jabbering, Lalla would make me learn the collect for the day. Sadly there is not one single collect that lodged permanently in my memory.

Lalla was a happy, loving and easy-going person, despite many sadnesses in her life – the loss of her father when she was only 5, the banishment of her eldest son Charles to Australia, her permanent exile from the land of her birth, long separations from her husband, the loss of three other sons between 1914 and 1918; two within a month of one another as a result of war injuries. Perhaps she looked upon me as a substitute son.

It was not until I was quite old, that I realised how ingrained South Africa was in Lalla. As a child, when I went shopping with her, it struck me that she modified her intonations when she spoke to the shopkeepers. Of course, I realized later, she naturally had a South African accent, which she tried to disguise when speaking in public. She was, in fact, ardently pro-British. I remember her scolding Tommy (my father) for not standing up when the National Anthem was being played on the wireless (as the radio was then called). Incidentally, my dear grandfather, Lalla's husband, would stand up, in his old age, for *Land of Hope and Glory,* no doubt mistaking it for the National Anthem.

Chapter 4

# CHILDHOOD

It will be seen from a reading of the earlier chapters, that I am of very mixed descent, with traces of Scottish, English, French, Dutch, German and probably Indian blood. But, of course, I have always considered myself to be *British*.

I was born in a Nursing Home in Bedford on 25 April 1926; four days after the Duchess of York gave birth to her elder daughter Elizabeth (later to become the Queen). I was a late arrival. Jean (my mother) told me that the nurses chided her because the Duchess of York had beaten her to it. Many years later, I was surprised to discover that a second cousin, Isobel Mary King, (one of the Orr Sutherland family) was born in the very same nursing home, two years previously. Probably Lalla (my grandmother) insisted that my birth should take place in a nursing home, bearing in mind that Jean's first born, Nigel died a day after his birth.

Ninety twenty-six, the year of my birth, was the year of the General Strike. The strike was called by the general council of the Trades Union Council in an attempt to force the government to act to prevent wage reductions and worsening conditions for coalminers. The strike, which lasted for six days at the beginning of May, was unsuccessful. Tommy volunteered to drive a train on the London underground. After a few abortive attempts, he was able to stop his train with all the coaches alongside the platform. At first, either the leading coach or the tail of the train was left in the tunnel!

I was baptised in All Saints Church, Worlingham, Suffolk on 20 June 1926. Tommy gave his occupation as boat owner and his address as Musk Farm, Beccles. This house still stands. I have no recollection of what the house looked like in the 1920s, but today, it appears to me to be rather charming.

My first memory of a home is of Beacon Mill House in Benenden, Kent. By that time, Jean, Heather and I were living with Lalla. I remember Lalla's husband, my grandfather coming to Beacon Mill House, on one of his periodic visits from South Africa. Once he took Heather and me (I was in a push chair) on a seemingly long walk: could it possibly have been to or from Tenterden?

While we were living at Beacon Mill House, Lalla entertained a South African friend called Charlotte Albu. She was the sister of the then Bishop of Natal. Heather and I must have heard the family commenting on her size. We were sitting on the stairs when Charlotte arrived and was shown up to her bedroom. "You don't know who I am" said Charlotte. "Oh yes, we do" we replied. "You are the mountain of flesh"! Charlotte took it in good spirit.

I believe it was at Beacon Mill House that Jean showed Heather the Easter present she was to receive in a few days time, on the strict injunction that she was not to touch it. It was an imitation bird's nest with 6 or 8 chocolate eggs embedded in straw. Whilst Jean's back was turned, Heather picked up each egg in turn, bit the bottom end off, and returned it to the nest, right way up. It appeared that nothing had been touched. Heather was complimented on being such a good girl. Was the subterfuge discovered on Easter Day? I hope not, but I fear so.

If my memory is correct, we all moved from Beacon Mill House to Crowborough in Sussex when I was about 5. I do not know what prompted the move. We stayed first in a boarding house, then in a rented house called Jerningham and finally in another rented house called Little Wortham. Uncle Douglas came over from South Africa while we were living at Jerningham. Lalla painted the attic bedroom purple for him. He was brusque and school-masterly with Heather. She was shut in a room and told to read *Alice in Wonderland.*

Uncle Gordon came on a visit from India, with his wife Matilda, while we were living at Little Wortham. Jean and my two aunts were concerned that Lalla would be upset to find that

Matilda was Anglo-Indian. It has to be said that all three of Lalla's daughters were mildly racist in their outlook, a reflection of their South African birth and upbringing. I clearly remember Jean telling me that in her youth in East London (South Africa), an African would step off the pavement into the carriageway when passing a white woman. Moonie, in her final illness in hospital, could not bear to be tended by a black nurse. Be all that as it may, Matilda was a dear person and easily won our hearts.

Whilst Uncle Gordon was dozing in a hammock in the garden of Little Wortham, Heather and I gathered together a few twigs and dry leaves and lit a small fire underneath him. The smoke, of course, aroused Uncle Gordon. "Whatever are you up to" he said? Heather was quick on the uptake. "We thought that since you came from India, you might be feeling the cold"! Uncle Gordon got up and prepared a rather more splendid fire. It wasn't burning too well, so he fanned it. "Why are you doing that" I asked? "You will blow it out". "What would you do then" he replied? Like a fool, I said "spit on it". Uncle Gordon was great fun. He taught us many party and conjuring tricks.

Heather and I went to a kindergarten school in Crowborough, run by Archie and Dorothy Hollins. Archie was always called *Sir.* For example, one would say "have you seen Sir?" We called Dorothy *Mrs. Hollins.* Sir (Archie) suffered mildly from shell-shock, as a result of his experiences in World War I. It was Mrs Hollins, not Sir, who ran the school. She was the daughter of an Admiral. I got on well with her: Heather not so well, it would seem.

Sir did no teaching; Mrs. Hollins was assisted by the two Miss Edmondsons; the senior sister taught the older children and was called *Miss Edmondson,* the junior sister taught the younger children and was called *Miss Kathleen.* There were other female members of staff, employed on a temporary basis, but no male staff.

Heather is fifteen months my senior. She is, by nature, a loving and caring person. When we were both at Hollins's, she made it her mission to take good care of her little brother. I didn't have the same sweet nature. In fact, I was rather jealous of Heather. I thought, probably quite incorrectly, that she was her mother's favourite. On one occasion, we children were presented by some visitor or other with two table napkin rings. One was orange, the other was green. Jean said "Heather you are the elder, you choose first". I objected! Heather said "let Malcolm choose first". I thought to myself "Heather will surely prefer the orange coloured ring". I therefore said "I should like the orange ring, please". I was quite upset when Heather said "oh good! I wanted the green ring and now I have got it"! Was she being kind to me, or was she scoring a point? I still have that orange table napkin ring.

Probably because our mother was unwell at the time, Heather and I became weekly boarders at Hollins's. I was under the age of 6. It was always a great wrench returning to the school on Monday mornings. I tried to eat so much during the weekend that I would have a bilious attack on Monday and so be kept home for at least one more day. It didn't work. In retrospect, I was not unhappy at Hollins's. I enjoyed the company of the other children, some of whom had parents living abroad and stayed on at Hollins's during the school holidays. My particular friend was an Irish boy called Shaun Clapham. I had a crush on a girl perhaps two years my senior called Mary Blackwell – my first love affair! Mary's two siblings also went to Hollins's; a brother called Benjamin and a sister called Jennifer. Benjamin's middle name was Pears. The children's mother was a sister of the tenor Peter Pears.

I got into several scrapes at Hollins's. Once, after a pillow fight in the dormitory, I was trying to tack a paper picture back onto the wall above my bed. It had got torn down in the mêlée. Sir happened to be next door and heard the banging on the wall. He stormed in, pulled down my bedclothes and took a slipper to my bottom. More naughtily, I once hid the shoes of a younger boy in my dormitory, by placing them in the bottom drawer of his washhand stand. When he came down to breakfast he was told to return to his dormitory and put on his hoes. He shortly reappeared in tears. "I can't find them" he said. Eventually, I had to own up. My punishment was to be sent to bed for the day. The meals were adequate, I suppose, but there were several horrors that had to be endured – lumpy porridge, globs of rice and treacle, dried figs and so on. Everything had to be eaten up, however unpalatable. After I became a full time boarder, the big treat of the week was a banana and brown sugar for breakfast on Sunday.

The biggest omission from the school curriculum was ball games. There was a swing and a see-saw and a sand pit, and I can recall some attempts at French cricket on the lawn. But there was nothing else, not even kicking a ball around. When I moved on to my preparatory school, I found that other boys of my then age (8 or 9) were far more skilled at ball games than I was.

I do not believe that there is such a condition as *the innocence of youth.* My love for Mary Blackwell was quite platonic; not so the fumbles I indulged in with other girls in home-made chair-and-towel "houses". In particular, I remember the pleasure of fondling the breasts of one girl in the dark corridor where we hung our overcoats. She enjoyed it, too! Not so exciting, in fact rather repulsive, was the invitation by one small boy – which I accepted – to take his penis in my mouth.

Whether or not my sexual exploits were noticed, it was thought that the time had come to move me from the kindergarten to an all boys' preparatory school. Heather stayed on at Hollins's for several more years; in fact for too long. She was 13 or 14 when she eventually moved on. She then became a boarder at an Anglo-Catholic girls' school at Baldslow near Hastings, called *St. Mary's.*

By now, World War II had started. After one term St. Mary's moved to Herefordshire. I believe Heather's education at St. Mary's cost very little. The nuns had hopes that she would stay on and teach there. But that was not to be. It was Frank de Jonge who got Heather into St. Mary's. He was an Anglo-Catholic priest, the son of great friends of Lalla. Like Uncle Douglas, he had been to Oriel College, Oxford. He was devastatingly good-looking.

Whether or not he had been in love with Douglas, or perhaps with Moonie, and was rejected, he turned his collar back to front and became a celibate priest.

Throughout his life, Frank de Jonge remained a good friend to all the family. Once when I was leaving London by train to Exeter on my return to my final school, Frank came to the station, saw me off and slipped half-a-crown into my blazer pocket (a generous present in those days). Many years later, Frank was the resident priest at a closed order of nuns in West Malling, Kent. My mother and I went to have lunch with him there. He was the only man whom the nuns were permitted to see. The food at lunch was brought to a closed hatch. There was a gentle tapping on the hatch door and after a discreet interval, Frank opened it and carried the food to the dining table. The nuns were not allowed to see me. Frank said there was a tale that the murderers of Thomas Becket stopped there (it was not a nunnery then) on the night following Becket's murder in Canterbury Cathedral. On every anniversary of the murder, it was said that you could hear the horses' hooves, as the murderers arrived. I am reminded of a visit I made to Canterbury Cathedral in the 1950s when two American ladies, standing at the very spot where Becket was murdered, asked the official guide "Gee! Do tell us, is this where they actually shot the film *Becket*"?

I have digressed. There was no money to pay for my private education, but no thought of sending me to a state school. The situation was saved by two strokes of good fortune. First and foremost, Uncle Douglas agreed to settle most of the bills. His financial assistance continued right through to the time I left my public school. When some years later, I was asked at an interview who had been the greatest influence on my life, I had no hesitation in replying "my uncle" (Douglas). His support was truly a remarkable act of kindness, which I never forgot. Indeed, in later years, when I was earning a reasonable salary. I am proud to say that I repaid Uncle Douglas the whole of his outlay.

The other stroke of good fortune which allowed me to get a place in a good preparatory school, at reasonable expense, arose like this. Our neighbour at Jerningham was a Miss Martineau. Her nephew, Hugh was a master at St. Hugh's School, Woodhall Spa, Lincolnshire. Thither I was sent at a reduced fee.

St, Hugh's School had been established by George Forbes in 1925. He was still the headmaster when I arrived. Forbes named the school after *Little St. Hugh of Lincoln*. Little St. Hugh was the son of a poor woman of Lincoln named Beatrice. He was born in 1246. The story goes that Hugh, aged nine, hit or threw a ball over a wall into the grounds of a Jew named Copin. A large number of Jews is then said to have tortured Hugh, scourged him, crowned him with thorns and crucified him in mockery of Christ's death. Beatrice went to Copin's house and discovered her son's body at the bottom of a well in his garden. Copin was accused of murder and confessed the crime. He said it was a Jewish custom to crucify a young boy once a year. Copin was put to a cruel death. Hugh's body was retrieved and buried in great state in Lincoln Cathedral. The martyrdom of Hugh became the subject of ballad poetry in the Middle Ages and miracles were said to have been wrought at the child's tomb. St. Hugh's School badge depicts a ball over a wall.

Sadly, St Hugh's School now dismisses the legend of *Little St. Hugh* and pretends that the school is named after Bishop St. Hugh of Lincoln, whose name day it celebrates. The school badge of a ball going over a wall, the current Headmaster says, is simply typical of a child at play.

I was most unhappy at St. Hugh's. For a start, I didn't take to Hugh Martineau who, in a sense, was my benefactor. He taught French. He was unattractive. He was boring. On one occasion he asked a boy to open a window and let in some fresh air. I quipped "and let out some hot air"! I wasn't reprimanded. Hugh encouraged me to read. He awarded me a Mars bar for the most interesting list of books read. Hugh had an attractive and charming wife called Grace. Grace was kind enough to invite me to tea now and again on Sundays. She gave me piano lessons and she played the harmonium at our daily prayers. I believe she had been an organist at Liverpool Cathedral. She dropped a little in my admiration when she told me – no doubt quite correctly – that I was singing a hymn out of tune. I had a reasonable treble voice and one Sunday I had to sing a solo in the church at Woodhall Spa, before the usual local congregation.

It was common knowledge amongst us boys that the headmaster, George Forbes had a crush on Grace. This didn't surprise us, because George's wife, Joan was far less attractive than Grace. Joan was a Watney. I think it was Watney money which helped George set up St. Hugh's in the first place. George was a meanie, particularly when it came to food. One could have toast and butter, or toast and marmalade, but certainly not toast, butter and marmalade*, all together.* The menu was uninspiring and the food was poorly cooked. The "big treat" on the last supper each term was a faux poached egg comprising half an apricot upturned on a little semolina.

Not only was George a meanie, he was also something of a disciplinarian. All sweets had to be handed in. They were then locked up and doled out frugally, six sweets only after lunch on Wednesdays, Saturdays and Sundays: nothing on other days of the week. On Sunday evenings, George would read to us. We had to sit in absolute silence, on pain of retribution. One poor boy was too overawed to ask to leave the room, during a reading session. The end result was that the poor lad wet himself.

George, however, did have quite a good sense of humour. On one occasion, when he was driving four of us boys to Trent Bridge to watch a Test Match, we passed a goat tethered on a village green with two policemen standing by wondering what they should do. George opened the window of his Citroën and called out "that makes **three** of you"!

There were two more members of the staff whom I can recall quite clearly. One was a master called Monk. Monk sometimes gave me a lift in his car, back to Sussex, at the end of term. The other was the PT Instructor called Sergeant Raw. Raw had been an army sergeant. He was a sadist. He took a great delight in making the more timid boys – of whom I was certainly one – perform exercises on the wooden horse, to our great terror, if not to our actual injury. He had us out in the public road (Cromwell Avenue), clad only in our vests and shorts, whatever the weather, for early morning physical exercises. His one redeeming feature was that he was a good carpenter and taught woodwork well. For many years, I had a wooden stool and a wooden cake-stand that I had made under his supervision.

*Sergeant,* as he was called, also coached us in boxing. This sport terrified me almost as much as attempting to vault the wooden horse in the gymnasium. However, I learnt one important lesson, namely that with enough determination and will-power, one can psych oneself to overcome any fear. I determined that I would not give way to my inward fears when faced with the prospect of a formal boxing match. The net result was that I boxed rather well and gained considerable confidence. A few years later, I even managed to knock out the senior cadet at my army OCTU (Officer Cadet Training Unit).

Matched in sadism to *Sergeant*, was the school matron. After we had got out of bed in the morning, we had to file past Matron, clad only in our pyjama trousers, lean over a bath of cold water and have her empty a large basin of this water over our shivering backs.

It was at St. Hugh's that I had my second big love affair! I fell in love with a girl who had some sort of housekeeping job at the school. I suppose she was in her late teens – at least 7 years older than I was! I forget her name. I have a vivid memory of sitting beside her, holding her hand, while George was showing us a film on his cine projector, one evening. My penis was throbbing in my shorts, the whole evening! (George once showed a film backwards, by mistake. This was a great success with the boys who frequently asked him to repeat the exercise).

A boy called Mawer told me the "facts of life". He emphasised the great pleasure in having an orgasm, which was beyond my powers at that time. Another boy called Stevens got his parents to take us out to lunch one Sunday. We went to Skegness. After lunch, Stevens persuaded me to walk into the shrubbery with him, where he wanted us to indulge in some mutual masturbation.

As far as I was concerned, it was unsuccessful. I didn't care for Stevens, in any case.

And that was my major problem at St. Hugh's. With one exception (Addison), I liked none of the boys. And they no doubt disliked me – with the possible exception of the kindly Addison. They were all sons of well-to-do Lincolnshire fathers. I had an impoverished father, whom I hardly knew, and came from south of the Thames. In other words, I was a duck out of water.

It was during one extended school holiday that I had my first, self-induced, orgasm. I was in bed recuperating from measles (I think it was) and being pampered by Nan Corfield. We were then living with Nan and her husband *Squawk* at Chick Hill Cottage in Pett (near Hastings). Nan was the most kindly of souls, a retired nurse who had in her care, and who was the source of her only income, a mentally retarded man of middle age called Colin Campbell. *Squawk* had a girl-friend at Bexhill – a dairymaid – to whom he paid regular weekly visits! But he never deserted Nan. She was devoted to him.

I remember that that self-induced orgasm was followed up by a passionate love letter to my beloved young housekeeper at St. Hugh's!

*

In terms of family moves, I need to retrace my steps. At about the time when I first went to St. Hugh's, the family (that is Lalla, my mother, Heather and I) went to Hastings for a Christmas holiday, at the Metropole Hotel (bombed during World War II). We then moved to Rosemary Cottage in Fairlight and from there to Summerhayes in Pett. At the Metropole Hotel, I embarrassed all and sundry by shouting out that the "boy" sitting on the entertainer's knee was false. The entertainer, of course, was a ventriloquist (not a very good one) and the "boy" was his dummy. I had no idea what ventriloquism was all about!

We experienced a very hot and dry summer at Rosemary Cottage. As a result, there was an acute water shortage. We children had to walk down the road and fill up buckets of water at the well of a local farmer. Heather and I also had to make use of the garden, in the manner of a cat! The mentally-retarded son of a local shopkeeper came occasionally to fill the lavatory cistern with buckets of water. He seemed to take a fancy to Heather, whom he petrified.

Rosemary Cottage was on the side of a steep hill. The occasional bus which passed by on its way to Hastings would labour up the hill with some difficulty. I used to run alongside it, and thereby made friends with some of the conductors. It was all rather fun, but we were not sorry to move to Summerhayes in Pett.

Summerhayes has an interesting history. It is semi-detached. The adjoining house was called Broadhayes in our days (but no longer). Two spinster ladies, Hilda Peace and Winifred Miller, both daughters of bank managers, won a competition organised by a national newspaper for the design of a house by amateurs. The prize was to be a building plot and the construction of the house. Hilda (Broadhayes) and Winifred (Summerhayes) won the prize. From the road frontage, the building appeared to be one house. Immediately in front of the centre was a small thatched rondavel-type building which housed a hand pump in the form of a large wheel, situated over a well. The well supplied the water to each house. On both flanks of the building there were small extensions housing built-in garages. At the rear of the building, it became evident that there were two dwellings, not one, because a hedge separated two gardens. Each dwelling had three bedrooms.

Hilda (known to us as Aunty Peace) and her father (Gramps Peace) lived in Broadhayes. Lalla rented Summerhayes from Winifred Miller. The Peaces were wonderful and kindly neighbours, especially to us children. I was invited to play their piano at any time. Gramps called me Paderewski (which he pronounced Paderooski). Gramps had a car. We had none. Gramps would take us children on an occasional outing. Once we went as far as Canterbury. On that journey, Gramps handed me the AA Guide and invited me to select any town named in it. He would then tell me in which county the town lay. All his answers were correct.

I am sure Aunty Peace would have liked to have had children of her own. On one occasion, her nephew Peter and niece Nancy came to stay with her. Peter took a great fancy to Heather. Nancy was several years my senior. There was no spark between us!

We shared a gardener with the Peaces. It was he who pumped the water up to our attic water tanks. The grown-ups called him *Smith.* But when Heather and I followed suit, we were instructed to call him *Mr.* Smith! Frank Smith worked one day a week for us and 4 days a week for Gramps, who had extended his garden by buying some land from the farmer who owned the adjacent field. Gramps was a keen gardener, whose garden was far more beautiful than ours.

We also had a maid. She was called Alice Catt. She came by bicycle on weekdays. She wore a black dress with white apron and starched cap. I hope I didn't embarrass her when one day she said "I must just put the 'ash in the h'oven" and I responded "the ash must surely be raked out from under the oven and put in the dustbin".

At Summerhayes, grandfather – who, by then, had retired from South Africa – occupied the front bedroom. This became my bedroom after grandfather moved into a nursing home in St. Leonard's, towards the end of his life. Before that, I shared one of the back bedrooms with Lalla, while Heather shared the other back bedroom with our mother. I recall numerous weekends when either Beaunes or Moonie came down from London, sometimes with a friend. For the life of me, I cannot recall what the sleeping arrangements were then, but there were certainly overnight stays, because I remember sewing up the trouser ends of one guest's pyjamas and putting Epsom salts in the chamber pot under the bed of another guest.

On summer visits, there were always long walks – across the fields, along the cliff top, over the "firehills" at Fairlight and so on. I don't remember my mother or Lalla joining us: they probably stayed at home, engaged in domestic duties. On one or two occasions, Tommy was a visitor. In particular, Lalla asked him to come and eradicate the rats which the previous tenants had encouraged by placing food for the birds on the back lawn. Traps were set in the hedge which divided Summerhayes and Broadhayes, but all that was caught in the traps was a hedgehog. The poor thing didn't die outright, but spent the rest of the night howling just like a baby, until it was finally dispatched. Tommy then shot at least one rat near the garden compost heap.

Pett was, and still is, a small elongated roadside village. When we lived there, it boasted a church, a rectory (since gone), a village shop, butcher, post office, builders' yard and pub. Gramps and Aunty Peace didn't care for the church (or perhaps it was the rector, Mr. Moxon) and went regularly to Fairlight Church. We patronised Pett Church – irregularly!

Now and again, Heather and I were invited to children's parties at the rectory. We hated those parties. We tried our best to get out of going to them, once to the extent of pretending we were on the phone to the rector to tell him "I'm very sorry, but Heather and Malcolm will be unable to come to your party tomorrow evening".

The Church Warden lived in Mill Cottage (later rented by us). He was called Major Lewes. He had a most attractive, much younger "wife" and a young baby. Heather and I had to call on him, for some reason or other. When he came to the door, his fly buttons were undone. We reported this gleefully to my mother. She immediately dubbed him *the fly-blown major*! Alas, all was not as it seemed. It became known that the fly-blown major had deserted his wife. The person we thought was his beautiful young wife was, in fact, the governess to previous children. The new baby was his by the governess. Today, this might pass without adverse comment. But in the 1930s it was a great scandal: a church warden, no less, living in sin. The fly-blown major and the pretty governess had to leave the village. I hope they both found happiness elsewhere.

The man who kept the village shop called on Lalla each week, took her order and then delivered her groceries in his van. We children sometimes walked or bicycled the length of the village to the village shop in order to buy my mother a packet of 20 cigarettes (less than 5p.), or to get some item that Lalla had forgotten to include in her weekly order. Biscuits were not sold in packets, as they are today, but were weighed out from large tins into paper bags, as required. The butcher once had to store and butcher an impala, shot in South Africa by Uncle Douglas and then shipped to England.

The post mistress was Mrs. Colegate. We thought the world of her. Her father had been the last miller at the nearby Icklesham Mill. I opened a savings bank account in the post office, in which I deposited much of my pocket money. After the death of both Lalla and my grandfather, my mother Jean was in greatly reduced circumstances. I drew out most of my savings to help her.

Grandfather would take a bus into Hastings for a daily shave by a barber. He often bought safety razor blades, well beyond his needs for his Sunday shave at home. Lalla preferred to hire the local taxi for the occasional shopping expedition to Hastings. It was a great treat to go with her, because we would always have elevenses at Cave's Café, which included live string music and – for me – a chocolate biscuit. Mr. Maitland ran the taxi service: in fact, a private car. He would take us to Hastings, wait for us and then bring us home to Summerhayes, all for a fee of 25p, (including a tip). Maitland, as the grown-ups called him, wore the same clothes week in and week out, throughout the year. He had a theory that one needed as many clothes to keep the heat out in summer, as one did to keep the cold out in winter. He was a *gentleman,* in the old-fashioned sense of the word; an ex-public school boy who had fallen on hard times.

After the death of my grandfather in 1939, there was no more income coming in from the firm of *McJannet & Co.*, in East London. There was only a small inheritance divided equally between all the living children. The firm, itself, was taken over by Uncle Bertie. Jean had to terminate our lease of Summerhayes. We boarded for a while with Nan Corfield at Chick Hill Cottage. Some of our household goods were stored in packing cases in Nan's semi-detached garage, a few hundred yards higher up

Chick Hill. They were pilfered – we believed by Canadian troops – and we lost most of the family silver. The thieves also broke into the adjoining garage, found nothing of any value and so, for the fun of it, nailed our packing cases to the party-wall.

One valued possession which survived was part of a Crown Derby fruit service, decorated with hand-painted flowers. Lalla had owned a complete service of 12 plates and 3 fruit dishes. After she died, the set was divided between her 3 daughters, Jean, Beaunes and Moonie. I inherited Jean's four plates and one dish. When Moonie died, her widowed husband, Harold Mills, very kindly gave me Moonie's complement of four plates and one fruit dish. In her old age Beaunes, who was generous to the point of fool-hardiness, (the porter at Chelsea Cloisters in London, where Beaunes lived, was a frequent recipient of gifts) repeatedly asked me to take whatever of hers I would like. I would have loved to have been given the remaining four plates and one fruit dish, thereby restoring the service to a complete set. But naturally, I refused all her offers and said "you must enjoy all your possessions for as long as you can". When Beaunes was removed to hospital (on the first occasion: she later died in another hospital), I plucked up courage and asked her husband, Audley if I could perhaps buy her four Crown Derby plates and fruit dish. Alas, Beaunes had already given them away, whether to the porter at Chelsea Cloisters, or more probably, as a wedding present to one of Audley's aristocratic relatives – of whom he seemed to have many. When Heather's younger daughter Rosemary married, some years later, I was able to give Rosemary only eight plates and two fruit dishes, as a wedding present.

*

I have digressed. My mother, Heather and I moved from Chick Hill Cottage to Mill Cottage, which came onto the leasehold market at a reasonable rent, after the fly-blown major quit the village. We were living at Mill Cottage when Neville Chamberlain announced that Britain was at war with Germany. It was 11 o'clock on Sunday 3 September 1939. The air-raid sirens sounded in Hastings only a few minutes after Chamberlain's broadcast. We all thought that a gas attack was imminent. The maid from the rectory rushed to the church in order to give the rector his gas mask. It was a false alarm. Nevertheless, next day I was sent to *Baldwins*, the local builder, to buy puttee for sealing any cracks in the window frames.

A more sensible safety measure was to protect one's windows against splintering caused by bomb blast, by gluing netting onto the panes of glass. Otherwise, shards of glass could possibly fly in all directions. Even the windows in the carriages of the underground trains in London were protected in this manner. There was a cartoon in an underground train carraige of a man trying to peel away the netting. It bore the caption "I hope you'll pardon my correction. That stuff is there for your protection". A wag had scribbled underneath "Thank you for this kind information. But how do I see the bleeding station?" In those days there were no loud speakers or display signs in carriages which gave the names of stations.

Pett was on the edge of Romney Marsh, which was deliberately flooded during World War II, as a security measure. People were cajoled, if not obliged to leave the area if they could. My mother, Heather and I went to London – on the face of it, a more dangerous place than Pett. But in London, Jean was able to secure accommodation and a housekeeping job with an old family friend, Kathleen (K) Bryham. K ran a rented room establishment in Manchester Street, W.1. She was a delightful person, prone to having rather too many gins, but full of gaiety and kindness. During school holidays (perhaps no more than two) I slept on a settee in K's basement. Many cockroaches scuttled around if the lights were put on in the middle of the night. K had had a sad deal in life. Maurice, her husband, had deserted her for a barmaid. Their only son, an army officer, was reported missing in Burma, and K never discovered what his actual fate was. He certainly must have died. K was adept at the occasional spoonerism. She said "Malcolm, you really must read T.E. Lawrence's *Seven Pissers of Willesden*"! On another occasion she said "I don't like going into the bedroom of that Roman Catholic priest. It always smells of *incest*"!

From K's we moved to the house of Heather's godmother in Ealing. I was probably about 16 years old then. Amelia Wedderspoon was an evangelical, aged spinster, as narrow as you can find them. The Wedderspoons had been friends of the Sutherland family in India. It was as a result of this connection, that Tommy chose Miss Wedderspoon ("Weddy") to be one of Heather's godmothers. I believe Tommy also touched Weddy for a loan, which he never refunded. 45 Grange Road, Ealing, Weddy's home, was a typical London house, on 5 floors, including the basement. Weddy's bedroom was on the first floor. She insisted on having a hip bath in her bedroom, daily. Maria, her delightful Irish Catholic live-in maid/housekeeper was obliged to carry cans of hot water up from the basement, to fill her mistress's bath. She also had to carry up coals for all the bedroom fires. After taking her bath and dressing, Weddy would come tripping down the stairs to the dining room for breakfast, singing "All things bright and beautiful"!

Maria spoilt me. She would raid Weddy's well-stocked larder for tins of fruit or jars of jam which she would then give me for my tuck box when I returned to school.

Weddy suffered from flatulence after meals. She would sit on a chaise longue in the drawing room after lunch or dinner, discreetly raise one leg and pass wind. I was demonstrating this ritual to Maria when, in the process, I inadvertently passed wind myself. Dear Maria: she crumpled up with laughter.

Heather, my senior by fifteen months, was already beginning to use make-up. But she had to remove it before entering 45 Grange Road. Weddy told Jean "your daughter is a Jezebel"! Weddy gave me a bakelite stud box inscribed *A Stud in Hand is Worth Two under the Bed.* I still use it.

I had long left St Hugh's. In the autumn of 1939, just after the outbreak of World War II, I went to Dover College. Infancy and childhood gave way to adolescence.

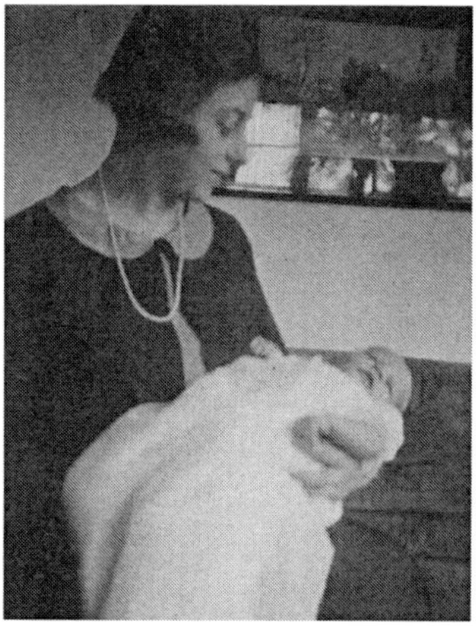

19. Author with Mother

20. Author (right) with Mother and Sister

21. Dorothy Hollins (boy not author)(1930s)

22. Mary Edmondson, Miss Broughton, Kathleen Edmondson (1930s)

23. Summerhayes (right) and Broadhayes (left)

24. Summerhayes –
Rear Elevation

25. Neighbours at Broadhayes – "Gramps" & "Aunty" Peace (1930s)

26. Alice Catt (1930s)

27. Frank de Jonge

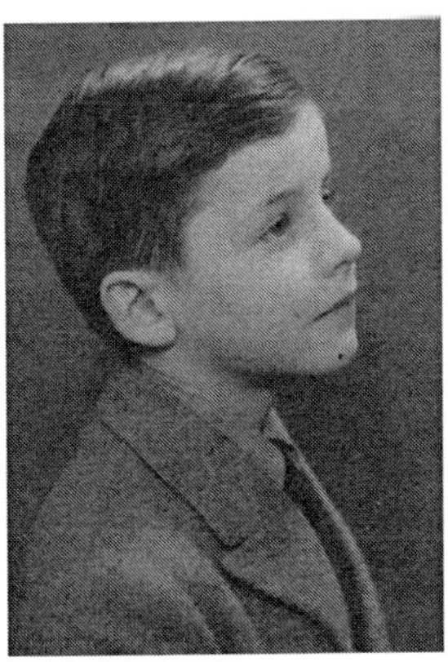

28. Author – off to St. Hugh's School

29. St. Hugh's School

30. Sparring – Author on left

31. Christmas Play
– Author as King

32. St. Hugh's Rugger XV 1939
– Author back row, second
from left

Chapter 5

# ADOLESCENCE

I got a scholarship to Dover College, after failing to get one to Haileybury. Haileybury had been the family's first choice of a public school for me, probably because of its connections with India. Dover College made a reduction in fees for the sons of army officers. Together with my scholarship, the net result was that my annual fees were reduced from £135 to £25. To this sum had to be added the cost of school uniforms and various extras. Uncle Douglas nobly footed the bills.

Dover College was founded in 1871. It occupied a large part of the grounds and old buildings of the Priory of St. Martin which had been ransacked by King Henry VIII at the dissolution of the monasteries. One school house was named *Priory House*; another was named *St. Martin's House*. The College was a boarding school for boys, but it also took in some day boys. There were no girls. The College did not become co-educational until 1974. The College motto was *Non Recuso Laborem* which we boys translated as "No! I refuse work". The proper translation, of course, is "I cannot refuse the task".

At the outbreak of World War II, the College closed Crescent House (which was the house for day boys) and evacuated to Devon. It joined up with Blundell's School. This was not a success. After one term, the College moved to Poltimore House, a stately home near Exeter. Poltimore had been the seat of the Bampfylde family for centuries. In 1831, the 6th Bampfylde baronet was ennobled as Lord Poltimore of Poltimore. The family continued to live in the house until 1920. It then became a girls' school.

Poltimore House underwent many alterations over the years. In its final 20th century form, the main south-facing front gave the appearance of a solid white stuccoed mansion. Some of the ground floor interior rooms were still of considerable magnificence when Dover College became the tenant. The entrance gate to the park was flanked by two huge balls on pillars. When I was the Editor of the College Magazine (*The Dovorian)*, a boy called J.M.E. Took penned a witty cartoon for the front cover which he entitled *How Lord Poltimore won his Balls*!

Many years later, I ran into Took again. He was then the Private Secretary to the Governor of Northern Rhodesia when I was the Deputy Commissioner of Lands there. Strangely, another Old Dovorian, J.C.A. (John) Mousley was also to become the Private Secretary to the Governor of Northern Rhodesia. Yet more strangely, John Mousley married the daughter of the Brigadier under whom I served in the Middle East.

Herne Bay College amalgamated with Dover College at the start of World War II, but even so the number of boarders dwindled alarmingly. It was a struggle for the headmaster, George Renwick to keep the College going and to bring it back safely to Dover when the war was over. Indeed, I believe George (as we called him – behind his back) subsidised the College out of his own pocket in order to keep it afloat. The whole time when I was at the College, it occupied Poltimore House.

What a wonderful transformation it was for me to move from St. Hugh's to Dover College. To start with, the food was a great deal better, despite the fact that it was war time. Far more importantly, I found myself – albeit a junior and a fag – in a small house (Leamington) where the boys were all friendly. As the school numbers dwindled, Leamington House was closed down. I moved to School House where I was equally happy. George was the housemaster of School House. George, his wife Isabel and their three children lived in a cottage converted from the stable block at Poltimore House. When I became more senior, a prefect and finally head boy of School House, George and Isabel would occasionally invite me to breakfast in their cottage. I had the greatest admiration for George. He was most helpful when I became the head boy in his house.

Being a fag lasted only for the first few terms. A prefect would shout **"Boy"** and all the fags would run to him, to ascertain his wishes. The last fag to arrive usually had some minor chore to undertake – perhaps to make the prefect toast, perhaps to clean his shoes, perhaps to carry a message to a prefect in another house, occasionally and bizarrely to warm up the lavatory seat for the esteemed bottom to sit on in comfort!

A 13-year old new boy, J.P (John) Hart, arrived in my house in the summer term of 1942. Many years later when John was a retired Brigadier, I got to know him well. He maintains that he once did a fag's errand for me! More flatteringly, John said I was the one boy who helped him settle in at his new school.

Prefects could impose *impositions* for any misdemeanour. An imposition might consist of learning a poem, working in the gardens, or writing out umpteen times "I must not . . ." For a gross misdemeanour, a boy might be whipped, either by his house prefects, more seriously by all the school prefects and most seriously of all by a master. I was certainly whipped twice by house prefects – I cannot remember why, but it may well have been for cheekiness. I have no doubt a caning was deserved. I don't think my canings did me any harm, but whether they harmed the prefects who administered them is another matter! I am proud to say that when in due course I became a prefect, I never once caned or participated in the caning of a junior boy. But like all the prefects, I certainly had a cane which, normally, I kept in my study.

I was still a duffer at all ball games. They were compulsory – cricket in the summer, hockey in the spring and rugger in the winter. Eventually I won both my rugger and my hockey colours, playing for the College. It was a case of "making up the numbers", I fear, not of any acquired prowess. My bête noir was cricket. When I became a senior boy, I managed to escape cricket by taking up rifle practice. Despite indifferent eyesight, I qualified as a *1st Class Shot.*

All school "honours" were faithfully recorded in the College magazine (*The Dovorian*) when one left, including whether one had become a 1st Class Shot. For several terms I edited *The*

*Dovorian*, but I resigned so as to let a contemporary have a go at the job. When I was the editor, I let pass, without correction, a misprint that a certain boy was a 1st Class Shit. And so he was, I might say!

School uniform was very formal when I first arrived: black pin-striped trousers, black jackets, starched collars with studs at the front and the back, black ties with a coloured stripe (purple for Leamington House, red for School House) and plain black ties on Sundays. All that soon changed. It was wartime. Formality gave way to the informal and far more sensible uniform of blazers and grey flannels. The headgear remained unchanged: white straw boaters with a black and white band for ordinary boys; black straw boaters with a black and white band for prefects. Although the school uniform was now more informal, a high standard of personal appearance was maintained. I recently saw a photograph of a group of boys at Poltimore making up their beds and cleaning the dormitory. It looked for all the world as if these boys were just going off to the city for a day at the office. Shoes had to be kept clean. Two prefects would stand at the chapel door, one on either side, when one entered the chapel for morning prayers. If a boy's shoes needed cleaning, he was in trouble. How sadly standards have now fallen.

The school chaplain was not, at that time, an ordained priest. So if one attended the Holy Communion service on a Sunday, one walked the length of a beautiful lime tree avenue to Poltimore village church. I sang in the College chapel choir and would sometimes play the piano for a service. There was a small organ, played by one of the staff, but it was frequently out of action. Before the harvest festival service one year, I stuffed a potato or two in the organ pipes, to dramatic effect! I don't think I was found out!

In addition to lessons and formal sessions of preparation (prep) in the evenings, there were compulsory games, compulsory chapel and many other activities, mostly of a voluntary nature. Because of a shortage of domestic and grounds staff (perhaps because it was war time, perhaps for reasons of economy) a great deal of cleaning and sweeping inside and of grounds maintenance outside was undertaken by us boys (compulsorily). Poltimore House in those days still had extensive grounds. It no longer has.

There was an Officers Training Corps in which I became a Sergeant. The highest rank open to a boy was Sergeant-Major-. Later I joined a contingent of the Home Guard. George was the enthusiastic officer in charge. We had many interesting exercises under his command.

There were also school plays and musicals. I took the part of Orsino, Duke of Illyria in *Twelfth Night* and the part of one of the three little maids in Gilbert and Sullivan's *Mikado.* There was an active and formal debating society, of which I became the President. One of my coups was to propose and win a motion that "this house **opposes** the nationalisation of industries" while simultaneously winning the Tower Essay Prize for an essay **advocating** the nationalisation of industries! (I played to the audience! The boys were budding conservatives: George, adjudicating the Tower essays, was leftward leaning)! I was also an enthusiastic member of the Gramophone Society. I spent many happy evenings listening to classical music played on a gramophone with a horn, vinyl records and fibre needles.

There had been no formal sex education at St. Hugh's. Before leaving for my first term at Dover College, Jean said "you do know the difference between right and wrong, Malcolm, don't you"? "Of course", I answered. There was no guidance from the absent Tommy.

It was during my first term at Dover College that I had my first genuine sexual experience with another boy. At lunch one day I was sitting on a bench beside F.G., who was slightly senior to me. Surreptitiously, under the table, he started fondling me. He encouraged me to do the same to him. We were soon in a state of some arousal, which I was urged to keep going until the meal ended. Then we both slipped quickly and quietly into a darkened cupboard where soon we both reached climaxes. I liked and enjoyed this novel experience, but was somewhat taken aback when F.G. gave me a big kiss when it was all over.

I cannot remember further encounters with F.G of a similar nature. I would have been a willing participant. I liked F.G. But I think that he rather liked playing the field: I was but one of his conquests!

Younger boys often had *crushes* on senior boys – the prefects or boys who had won their colours at games – and vice versa. I was an ardent admirer of G.G., but he was in another house and I am sure he never noticed me. M.N., on the other hand, took a great fancy to me when I was still a fag and he was a prefect. I warded off all his advances, which I found distasteful. But I am grateful to him for one thing: he warned me of the physical pitfalls and unpleasantness of anal penetration. As far as I am aware, there was no buggery in the school when I was there. Certainly, there was a good deal of masturbation, and at least some mutual masturbation. Perhaps this was only to be expected in an all-male environment, during adolescence. It seemed to be just part and parcel of growing up.

To be sure, I had several sexual encounters with boys of approximately my own age. One took place in the music room with C.F. He was considered to be an *s.m.* (a sexual maniac) As far as I was concerned; the encounter was not a success. Embarrassingly, I had a premature ejaculation. Far more satisfactory and entirely pleasurable was an episode with C.A., when we were sharing a bath one late evening (probably quite illicitly). I took a fancy to several other boys without success, and a few other boys seemingly took a fancy to me, with an equal lack of success. I certainly preferred to be the hunter, rather than the quarry. I continued to feel this way in later years, in hetero-sexual relationships. There is a certain frisson to the chase.

Finally, while I am on this theme, I have to say that I became passionately fond of P.J., when I was a prefect and he was a little younger than me. Our age difference was only two years. I was able to continue the affair during a school holiday: we happened to be living near one another at the time. When I left Dover College, the affair came to an end. It was also the end of all homosexual liaisons for me.

As at St. Hugh's, so at Dover College – there was no formal sex education. But just before I left the College, George took it upon himself to warn the departing boys "take my advice! Don't go rushing up to London and get involved with some prostitute or other. Always remember the danger of catching a venereal disease". In retrospect, I am not too sure whether this was good advice. We had been cooped up in an exclusively male environment for 4 or 5 years, when the only outlets for our sexual impulses were masturbation, wet dreams or homosexual affairs. We were sexual illiterates when we left the College. For some years to come, I found myself ill-at-ease in female company. A fling in London might have changed all this.

During my time at Dover College, Jean left London and got a succession of house-keeping jobs. The difficulty for her was that she had to find jobs in houses where there would be beds for Heather and me in school holidays. Sometimes this was not possible. A short-term job during school term would be followed by cheap holidays in rented accommodation. I recall staying in a farmhouse at Uplowman in Devon and, on another occasion, in a boarding house in Babbacombe, near Torquay.

We stayed in a succession of houses in Guildford. One of these was the home of the Hon. Mrs Lygon. Mrs Lygon knew neither how to make a pot of tea nor how to boil an egg. But she thought she knew the ways of little boys and accused me of removing the caster off my bed and taking it back to school with me! I remonstrated. Mrs. Lygon, to her credit, saw the folly of this accusation. She went and bought me a rather fine book of early poems by Tennyson, which I still have. Mrs Lygon had a cat called Henry. If the air raid sirens sounded after dark (remember it was still wartime), when not a chink of electric light was to be revealed, and Henry happened to be in the garden, Mrs. Lygon would fling open the front door, brightly lighting up the front garden and call out urgently "Henry! Henry! Do come inside".

At another house in Guildford, the owners had an obsession about conserving electricity. We were all meant to refrain from using lights in our bedrooms. But we had no intention of changing into our pyjamas in the lighted corridor. "Look at that! They have got their lights on again" would go up the cry. The son of the household worked in a local bank He was simple, but not so simple as to overlook the attractions of Heather!

During the summer holidays schoolboys were invited to volunteer for work on the land. This was seen as a contribution to the war effort. Farm labourers were in short supply after the requirements of the armed services had been met. For two successive summers, a group of 20 or 30 boys from Dover College, supervised by the school chaplain, helped on the farm of a widowed farmer living near the north coast of Devon. . I think it was not much more than a two-week stint on each occasion. The first summer when I volunteered, we were billeted in the NALGO camp at Croyde Bay: next summer, we were billeted in the village school at Braunton. It was delightful to have the marvellous sandy beach at Saunton Sands practically on our doorstep, but there was not much time to enjoy it! It was back-breaking work on the farm, after which one just wanted supper and bed. The husband of our widowed farmer had previously been a bulb farmer in Lincolnshire. He found that the sandy soils of his Devonshire farm were ideal for the culture of tulips, a crop with which he was familiar. Lifting tulip bulbs in the fields was extremely hard work. There was no mechanical aid. The furrows were turned over by a horse and one-blade plough. Then one had to grub through the upturned soil and lift each bulb by hand. A foreman made sure that none was missed! No sooner was one furrow cleared than the horse and plough came round to open up the next furrow.

During one summer holiday, instead of going to north Devon, I worked in a hop garden in Kent. Peter Thomas, with whom I shared a study at school, had an aunt who was the housekeeper to two elderly spinsters who owned a hop garden south of Maidstone. Peter's parents lived close by. They put me up. Peter worked in the oast house – a relatively exhausting job. I had the much easier task of being the "measurer". All the hops were picked by hand by families or groups of friends from the east end of London. They placed the hops in sizeable canvas bins. An overseer went round with a large basket emptying each bin. He called out, to me, the number of baskets collected from each bin. I then recorded that number in a ledger. Pay was on the basis of the number of baskets filled over the fortnight, or so, of hop-picking. During this fortnight, the principal worker in charge of a bin, could come to me and ask to draw out part of the money already earned. Then, at the end of the hop-picking season, the balance was paid out, by me – in cash. Some evenings, if Peter was not working in the oast house, we would play bridge with his parents. Peter became a life-long friend – and bridge became a life-long passion.

Of course, the prime function of schooling is formal education. I passed the School Certificate examination, aged just 15, with a sufficient number of distinctions and credits to exempt me from the Oxford and Cambridge matriculation examination. In other words, I was judged to be sufficiently well educated to go to university. However, I stayed on at Dover College in order to sit for the Higher School Certificate. For this examination one had to specialise in two subjects. I opted for Mathematics and History – a strange combination. Mathematics would normally be associated with one of the sciences, but I was a complete duffer at Physics and was not instructed in Chemistry. History, on the other hand, would normally be associated with another of the humanities – English Literature, perhaps. I think I simply picked two of the subjects for which I had gained distinctions in the School Certificate examination.

The sad truth is that I took academic pursuits far too easily after I had matriculated. There were so many more interesting activities in College life, away from the classroom. It also has to be said that the standard of teaching was poor. This came about because the younger members of the teaching staff went away to the war, and were replaced by old chaps who were not sufficiently up to it. Increasingly, I found Higher Mathematics beyond my understanding; I learnt it parrot-fashion. The net result of all this was that I ploughed the Higher School Certificate at the first attempt and only scraped through at the second attempt. By now I was aged 18. It was evident that I was not sufficiently bright to get a scholarship or exhibition to an Oxford or Cambridge college.

Nevertheless, I did go straight from Dover College to Selwyn College, Cambridge. This came about because I had volunteered to serve as an officer in the Royal Engineers. I was summonsed to attend a WOSB – a War Office Selection Board - which put one through one's paces for three or four days. I passed my WOSB. The army then sent me to Cambridge University to study for the first year Engineering course. This had to be crammed into six months, with no break, and with one day each week devoted to military training.

Conditions were arduous. All lectures **had** to be attended. One had to sign in at every prescribed lecture. Military training was under the direction of Captain de Braemeker – a sadist, if ever there was one. One poor lad got into great trouble for arriving late on parade. The fact that he had had a puncture of his bicycle tyre was not accepted as an excuse. He was punished.

Just before we had to take our final academic examination, de Braemeker had us out all one Saturday night building a Bailey bridge. The bridge was completed to perfection by the early hours of Sunday morning. De Braemeker strolled out of his hut, steaming cup of cocoa in his hand, and said "you made far too much noise building that bridge. That would have been fatal if the enemy had been close at hand. You will now dismantle it and rebuild it 50 yards downstream, in complete silence". We got back to our colleges after daybreak. Examinations loomed the following Monday.

A saving grace in our military training programme was the lectures by a typical warrant officer of the old school, who was too old for active service. He had a ready wit. "We are now" he said "going to learn all about piles for piers – and I don't mean 'aemorrhoids for h'aristocrats".

There was little time for us to engage in the usual activities at Cambridge University – punting on the river, partying, drinking coffee in the King's Parade engaged in friendly discussion or argument with other undergraduates. I did manage to get in just one game of rugger, and I founded a College play-reading society. We would meet one evening each week and read through a Shakespeare play, each of us taking the part of one or more of the characters. Occasionally I visited the College Master, George Chase who had a vast collection of gramophone records. He would ask what piece of classical music we would like to hear. Never once did he have to say "I'm sorry. I'm afraid I haven't got a recording of that".

I lived in College, sharing rooms designed for one undergraduate with another Royal Engineers cadet. We had little in common. All meals were taken in the College refectory, wearing undergraduate gowns. A senior undergraduate read a Latin grace before dinner every evening. When I paid a return visit to Dover College one day, as an old boy, I showed off by reciting this Latin grace before lunch – quite a contrast to the normal "For what we are about to receive etc". When I was a boy prefect at Dover College and it was my turn to say grace because a master wasn't present, I would say "On your marks, get set, go". It seemed appropriate when the two or three boys who got through the first course fastest might well get a second helping!

Like St. Hugh's and Dover College, Selwyn College in those days was an exclusively male institution. There was a ladies' college not far away (Newnham), but getting to know a girl was not easy. No girl attended our lectures, for example. No girl was training to become a Sapper officer.

While I was at Selwyn College, my school friend Peter Thomas was at Oxford University on a Naval Short Course. He invited me over to Oxford one weekend. I don't know quite how it happened, but we found ourselves dining with a peer of the realm and his male companion. We were probably "picked up" while we were having a drink at the Randolph Hotel. However, it became apparent during dinner that there was an ulterior motive behind their hospitality. Peter and I made an excuse to go to the lavatory and, from there, we rapidly escaped through a window.

On November 5th a considerable number of undergraduates took to the streets of Cambridge and ran wild. I saw a firework thrown into the entrance hall of a building occupied by American armed forces. I saw a car being overturned in the market square and set alight. The exuberance of youth, no doubt, but it was a disgrace. The university and city authorities feared a repetition of these disturbances on armistice night (November 11th). Extra police were drafted in from London and from Oxford. All was quiet! The unruly element had a good laugh!

Life at Cambridge was over all too soon. I had enjoyed it, despite the rigours and intensity of the Royal Engineers Short Course. I found myself a Private (not yet a Sapper) in the army. World War II was still being waged.

*

The initials of boys, as given in this chapter, are spurious, so as to avoid any embarrassment.

33. Poltimore House – Wartime Home of Dover College

34. Dover College Hockey XI – Author back row, centre

35. Dover College, War Effort (1943)

36. School House, Dover College, 1944 – Author next to George Renwick, Peter Thomas next to Isabel Renwick, John Mousley third row on right

37. Selwyn College Cambridge – Old Court

38. Selwyn College Cambridge – Chapel

39. RE Short Course Cambridge University 1944 – Author 3rd row 4th from right Maude behind de Bremaeker's left shoulder, Watson front row 4th from left

Chapter 6

# THE ARMY

There is a song which goes:

We joined the navy to see the world
And what did we see?
We saw the sea!
We saw the Atlantic and the Pacific . . .

I joined the army to serve my country in time of war. What did I see? I saw no active service. The war in Europe was drawing to a successful close. I was never posted to the Far East, where the war dragged on until America dropped its atomic bombs on Japan. But I did see something of "the World". In the space of three years' service, I had at least six different postings in England. Abroad, I saw service in Egypt (in two different locations), Italy and Palestine.

Coming down from Cambridge in March 1945, I became a Private, on the princely pay of 3 shillings (15p) a day. I was posted to Shrewsbury for a short course of "primary" training. This consisted of square-bashing, rifle and bayonet drill and the like. It really was a waste of time. There was nothing I learnt which I hadn't already picked up in the OTC, Home Guard or the Royal Engineers Short Course at Cambridge.

One benefit was that we were given medical and dental inspections and a series of inoculations in case we were posted to less salubrious climes. Before the inoculations, a Medical Officer gave us a lecture on why they were necessary. Good heavens! Some strapping young men fainted during the lecture. And when we paraded with our shirt sleeves rolled up, prior to receiving the necessary jabs, there were some more teenagers fainting long before they got to the head of the queue.

When it came to my dental inspection, the Dental Officer seemed far more interested in chatting up his (female) ATS assistant. "Everything is fine" he said. "But", I remonstrated "before I enlisted my dentist at home told me that I needed three small fillings, which he couldn't do for me before my call-up". The Dental Officer looked in my mouth again. Whether or not he found the cavities, he drilled away for a while and made some fillings, chatting all the while to the ATS assistant. Next day I declined to salute the Dental Officer when I walked past him. I was obliged to peel potatoes in off-duty hours!

The next step was Corps training, which is learning how to become a good Sapper in the Corps of Royal Engineers. I was no longer a Private. I became a Sapper My pay went up by one (old) penny a day. There must have been a delay before my next posting, to Clitheroe, because I was promoted to Lance Corporal and given a job in the stores. What I then did has weighed heavily on my conscience ever since. I became a petty thief. I raided another man's kitbag which was in the stores, stole a pair of his new socks and substituted an old pair of my own.

Shortly afterwards, I joined 141 War party, at Clitheroe. I was still a Sapper. The War Party was a group of young men, mostly, if not all, with a university background, who had been ear-marked to become Sapper officers. We were quartered in an old cotton mill which had been condemned in the 1920s as unfit for women to work in. There we were living and sleeping in this mill in the 1940s! The river Ribble ran through the basement of the mill. The walls were wet and covered in lichen. The sanitary provisions were foul. On top of all this, it seemed to rain every day.

I became friendly with two Old Etonians: Watson, whose father was a baronet with coalmining interests in Scotland; and Maude, who touched me for ten shillings (50p), which he never repaid!

Before long I and many others succumbed to an epidemic of scarlet fever. Off I went to an isolation hospital. I felt so ill, I really thought my number was up. But I recovered and was sent to an excellent convalescent home in a stately building in Lytham St. Anne's, belonging to the Clifton family. We dressed in hospital blues, instead of khaki. Naturally, the locals were unable to distinguish between those men recovering from wounds or injuries received in action, and the likes of me, recuperating after contracting an infection. Once, this became an embarrassment. I was waiting at a bus stop for a bus to take me into the town, when a middle-aged man at a bus stop on he other side of the road darted across the road and stuffed a ten shilling note (50p.) into the top pocket of my hospital blues. Clearly, he thought I was recovering from war wounds. I tried to refuse this spontaneous and most generous gesture, but before I could make any explanation, the goodly soul darted back across the road, boarded his bus and continued on his journey. This was a shining example of the sheer goodness, kindness and camaraderie found among so many people during the war years.

Once my health was fully restored, I returned to the dreaded Clitheroe and joined 147 War Party. Conditions had not changed. There were new friends to make. I became particularly friendly with Johnny Watts. He was an old boy of Mill Hill School. He had an amazing repertoire of what might politely be described as barrack room songs. Whatever went on at Mill Hill School?

We would queue up for our pay on Fridays and blow most of it in the local pubs on Friday evenings. I hope our behaviour wasn't so bad as to upset the Clitheroe locals. After one drinking spree, I became a little amorous towards one of the Northern Ireland lads who had been to Queen's University, Belfast. Johnny Watts, bless him, stopped me from making a fool of myself.

The training was rigorous, to the point of sadistic brutality. The assault course was a real horror, incorporating such features as crossing the river Ribble on a single suspended rope, with live ammunition and gun-cotton primers popping off in all directions. It was said that no questions were asked if casualties (even fatalities) were kept to a low percentage! Somehow, we all survived.

Another horrendous exercise was kit inspection, of which there were several. Every item of kit had to be laid out on one's bed to a prescribed pattern, all in perfect condition and all aligned the length of the sleeping quarters. "Perfect condition" was carried out to ridiculous extremes. The studs in one's boots had to be polished, as did the needles in one's housewife. The string attaching the cork of the water bottle to the bottle itself had to be secured with a knot called a fisherman's bend. No other knot would do. The cover of one's AB64 (an identification document) had to be polished with brown polish. And so on! One had to rise very early to make sure that every item of equipment was just so. Some anxious men slept on the floor after laying out their kit late at night.

Once, there was a kit inspection before we went on weekend leave. It was a real trial, because the previous day we had become muddied and wet through on the assault course. A man with the same surname as mine had tried – rather too successfully – to dry out the boots he had been wearing, by placing them beside the barrack room stove. Alas, he burnt a sizeable hole in one sole. Nothing daunted, he polished them up, put them on and laid out the spare pair of boots on his bed, polished studs and all. Surely no one knew of his dilemma! But the inspecting officer asked to see the soles of the boots poor David Sutherland was wearing. His weekend leave was cancelled. Many years later I looked up Sutherland in the *Army Lists*. I was pleased to see that he got his commission.

There was a second WOSB (War Office Selection Board) to be faced before becoming an officer cadet and going to OCTU in Newark. Again the WOSB lasted three or four days. There were numerous tests of intelligence, ability and initiative. For the whole time one was under a close watch by an officer on the Selection Board. One wondered if he was determining whether one comported oneself in a manner becoming to an "officer and gentleman"! In spite of making something of a bosh shot in re-assembling a bicycle pump which had been stripped down into its component parts, I passed my second WOSB. Off to OCTU I went.

Before we had completed our OCTU training, we were told that the Corps of Royal Engineers no longer wanted field engineering officers. We were required to apply for one of the specialist branches of engineering. I chose surveying, that is to say map-making. The officer who interviewed me asked "what do you intend to do after the war is over Sutherland"? I replied "join the Colonial Service, Sir". It was the right answer. He had been in the Colonial Survey Service himself. The interview degenerated into a long friendly chat. My application was successful.

Further training was necessary before one could be commissioned as an officer in the Survey Branch of the Sappers. The successful applicants were whipped away from OCTU and sent to the School of Military Survey. This was housed in prefabricated buildings in the grounds of Longleat. I found the training most interesting. I made new friends, in particular a rather wild Irishman called Andy Heron and an Old Marlburian called Arnold Phillips. Johnny Watts was also one of our number.

Andy Heron had a motor bike. Many times I was his pillion passenger. We favoured a particular pub in a village near Warminster. The landlady was called Mrs. Payne. She had two pretty daughters. Peggy, the elder daughter, had a young baby, reputedly fathered by an American G.I. We all fell in love with the younger daughter, Rosemary. Dear Mrs. Payne liked us. She didn't take to the more snobby infantry officers from Warminster, who were often booted and spurred. Mrs Payne would sometimes invite us Cadets into her private parlour, for a night-cap, after closing hours. As a result, one evening Andy and I and his motorbike ended up in the ditch! There was no real damage.

My other cadet friend, Arnold Phillips later served in Egypt at the same time as I did. We became lifelong friends. I am the godfather of his only son.

We were commissioned as Second Lieutenants during the course of our training at the School of Military Survey. There was a big celebration the evening before: drinks before dinner, a good hotel dinner with wines, and then off to Mrs. Payne's pub. There, I am ashamed to say, I drank seventeen glasses of port. Was I ill afterwards? Deservedly so!

Before our course ended, we were invited to say to which of several specified theatres of operation we would like to be posted. The three options were East Africa (Kenya), the Middle East (Egypt) and Germany. The war in Europe was over, so Germany meant joining the occupying Army of the Rhine. Johnny Watts opted for this. I thought it was a bit tame. After all, Germany was on our doorstep. My first choice was East Africa, but I was happy to settle for the Middle East when it was offered.

Soon I was ordered to report to GHQ Middle East in Cairo. We crossed the channel, made a train journey across France (four of us playing bridge practically non-stop) and boarded a troop ship at Hyères. It was Friday, 13 December 1945. The crew, being superstitious sailors, did everything in their power – so it seemed – to delay our departure to Saturday 14$^{th}$. They were unsuccessful. Lo and behold, the ship's engines broke down, halfway to Port Said. We bobbed up and down, at anchor, while the necessary repairs were being effected. I often wonder whether the engine failure was deliberately contrived by a superstitious sailor!

Eventually, Port Said hove into view. There was an off-shore wind blowing. The unsavoury smell of Egypt was overpowering. Ashore, that smell seemed to be ubiquitous, even pervading one's bedding. One got used to it. The Survey Directorate at GHQ was quartered at Maadi, on the outskirts of Cairo. I saw little of the city. On Christmas Day I attempted a round of golf with my good friend and fellow officer Rab McEwan. I knew that, in general, I was poor at ball games, but I thought my golf wasn't too bad. I had played a lot at Lundin Links while holidaying with Moonie, as a schoolboy. I soon found that I was now hopeless at that game, as well. Rab trounced me.

How is it that Rab and I were invited to the home of a friendly Egyptian? I believe he had offered to take us to the cinema in Cairo. He was a youngish man, with a wife and child. But it was soon all too clear that his interest in us was homosexual. We hurriedly escaped.

I worked in the Map Library, cataloguing. I was astounded

at the large number of editions of maps of the western desert, which we had published during the campaign. Not only was the land form constantly changing, in line with climate changes, but so were features such as abandoned tanks or burnt-out vehicles. For airborne troops, we printed maps on fine linen and even on silk.

It was not long before my Brigadier H.A.L. (Tony) Shewell told me that I was to be posted to Italy to join a Field Survey Company stationed at Lonigo, near Vicenza. I had to fly to Rome. There was engine trouble with the Dakota aircraft, before it took off from Heliopolis. Finally, we became airborne in the early hours of the morning. It was the first time I had flown. I was the only officer passenger. More engine trouble developed as we headed west over the desert. We touched down at El Adem for further checks. Then we headed north, across the Mediterranean. Soon there was yet more engine trouble. One of the two engines failed completely: the other wasn't sufficiently powerful for us to maintain height. Slowly we lost height and the Mediterranean loomed closer and closer. I cannot believe that it could have made much difference to our performance, but the RAF crew ordered us to jettison all our kit, including rifles, and finally the bucket seats on which we had been sitting. I had a heavy cold and was wearing my trench coat, with my greatcoat over my knees. I was told I must jettison one of my two coats. I opted to keep my greatcoat. Out went my trench coat – with all my handkerchiefs in the pockets. A naval ship was ordered out from Malta to pick up any survivors should we land in the drink. But with commendable skill and some luck, the pilot managed to reach Malta where he flopped down on the nearest airstrip.

All I had were the clothes I stood up in. But I was alive: not dead nor half-drowned. I was allocated sleeping quarters. The first thing I did was to tear off the bottom of one of the sheets and make half a dozen handkerchiefs out of it. In a while, washing and shaving kit and a change of clothing were provided. For four days the ground mechanics worked on our crippled Dakota. Then they deemed it fit for flight again. To his credit, our RAF pilot took off and tested out the plane. All was well. A few hours later, we landed safely at Rome.

Jean claimed that she had a premonition that I was in grave danger. She was mightily relieved to hear of my safe arrival in Italy.

I believe the sole purpose of my posting to 19 Field Survey Company was to assist in running down the Company. An officer was needed to take the few remaining men and all the equipment back to Egypt. All the current officers were due to be demobilised.

The men were quartered in the town of Lonigo: the officers' mess was in a rather pleasant villa some distance from the town. It was still winter. There was some local cross-country skiing. Those who had leave due to them repaired to Cortina for the real thing. The officer in command was Captain W. (Bill) Enderby - a nice enough man, but no leader. Everything seemed to be left to the non-commissioned officers – a grand bunch. Bill had an Italian girlfriend, who was a nightclub hostess. She was a pretty young thing. Bill sometimes brought her back to the mess. I had to tread very carefully: it seemed that she preferred me to Bill!

In due course, the Company was run down. A large convoy of equipment with me and a few men headed for Trieste, where we were to embark for Port Said. I must now make another confession. I was staying in a small hotel. After a day or two, I discovered that our ship had been loaded and was due to sail shortly. I hadn't been warned. There was time enough to pay my bill, but I hurriedly packed my bag and headed for the quayside, without saying good-bye **and** without settling my bill. This still troubles my conscience.

My men and all our equipment were duly discharged at Port Said, but I was ordered to escort other troops (nothing to do with my Company) to Suez. This caused some confusion.

While I was in Italy, GHQ Middle East had moved out of Cairo, in pursuance of an agreement reached between Britain and the Egyptian Government in 1936. Britain's major strategic interest in Egypt was the Suez Canal – a lifeline to India. Consequently GHQ moved to El Fayed, on the shores of the Great Bitter Lake. There was virtually nothing at El Fayed before the army arrived. Soon there was an extensive tented city and a few more permanent buildings. The latter included a shopping centre and a yacht clubhouse. It seemed to me that much of the work was being undertaken by, or under the supervision of German prisoners of war awaiting repatriation. My batman was a German POW. He looked after me well, but was inclined to nick my cigarettes.

We had to show our passes before entering the Headquarters office area. The guards on duty were German POWs! I sometimes played bridge in the evenings with a Colonel in Intelligence. He told me that once he showed the POW guard on the gate the papers belonging to the Beast of Belsen. The guard recognized the Colonel, saluted and let him pass. The poor guard got into some trouble.

In the Survey Directorate I worked alongside Captain Northover. Our remit was anything to do with air surveys. I became a member of JAPIC – the Joint Air Photographic Intelligence Committee. There were several survey officers senior to Northover, responsible for other survey activities, such as the printing of maps.

The second-in-command was Colonel E.H. (Tommy) Thompson. He had a brilliant brain. He was soon fluent in Arabic. In any discussions I had with Colonel Tommy, I was left far behind, but he never made me feel foolish. After the war, he became a Professor at London University. He invented the Thompson air photographic plotting machine.

The officers had frequent (daily?) conferences with the Brigadier, Tony Shewell. Shewell had a notice on his desk saying "A Committee is a group of people who, individually, have no power to get anything done. But, collectively, they are able to decide that, in the event, nothing **should** be done". (This might be a slight paraphrase).

When Northover was demobilised, Shewell sent for

me and told me that I was to take over all Northover's duties. However, I would not be promoted to Captain (I was then a full Lieutenant), because Rab McEwan was my senior and should be promoted before me. Shewell said, however, that when the next captaincy became available, **I** should be considered for it.

Rab McEwan, Arnold Phillips, David Griffiths (other young survey officers) and I had a marvellous time at El Fayed. In particular, Arnold and I became active members of the Yacht Club and spent many happy hours sailing on the Great Bitter Lake. The Lake was non-tidal, saline and with warm water – ideal for swimming, as well as yachting. After I left the army, Rab McEwan and I went sailing off the Isle of Wight. What a difference to sailing on the Great Bitter Lake, not least in coping with the tide.

Office hours in Egypt were from 8 a.m. to 12 noon and from 5 p.m. to 8 p.m., or thereabouts. Afternoons were available for sports, or for Egyptian PT (siestas)!

Unfortunately there was a shortage of British girls at El Fayed, but it seemed to me that we young survey officers had kraaled the three most charming girls. I am happy to say that Rab McEwan and David Griffiths walked off with – and eventually married – two of them. Having experienced an all-male education, I still found it difficult to enter into a serious relationship with a girl.

*

A vacancy for a captaincy soon came and off I went to Jerusalem to become Staff Captain Survey at HQ Palestine. My colonel, Arthur Walmsley-White (W-W) was an easy going man and we soon established a good friendship. He was an excellent photographer. He was also an avid student of Middle Eastern history and culture.

We had a Survey Company stationed in Transjordan (as Jordan was then called). W-W used that as an excuse to go on safari. Together W-W and I went to Petra. This was long before Petra became a major tourist attraction. Indeed, when we saw the rose-red old city, there were only the two of us, a couple of Sappers and an Arab guide. After seeing Petra, we crossed the

Sinai Desert in our jeeps and went to Luxor – again, completely without tourists at that time. What a memorable trip it all was, recorded by W-W in many beautiful photographs which I still have. W-W was a regular army officer. He later became a Brigadier. I stayed with him and his wife in England, after I had been demobilised.

*

At about the time I was posted to Palestine, Britain announced that it intended to cede its mandatory powers for the governance of Palestine to the United Nations. A date in May 1948 was set for the British withdrawal. The United Nations decided that Palestine should then be partitioned into an Arab state and a Jewish state. That was a decision of expediency. It made no sense in terms of geography, economics, or ethnicity. It appealed neither to the indigenous Arab community (still in a majority), nor to the wave of Jewish immigrants who had been promised a homeland in Palestine. But the Jews, with strong United States urging, accepted the proposition of partition. It gave them a foot in the door.

Arabs and Jews were at one another's throats. Both regarded the British as an irritant, an unwanted occupying power. It was difficult for the British army and police to hold the peace.

Life for the army in Jerusalem itself was not too pleasant. The old city was out of bounds. We never went out without at least one companion. Officers carried their revolvers the whole time. Revolvers were even placed under pillows at night. One evening at dinner in the mess, a flare went up. I continued eating my soup. More experienced officers immediately drew their revolvers, leapt from the table and crouched beside the wall of the mess. As it happened, it was a false alarm; a cat had touched a trip wire.

We drew up a map showing how Palestine was to be divided. We handed over. We left. I was on the last army convoy to leave Jerusalem. We headed for Egypt. We hadn't travelled far before we saw quite intense fighting between Arab and Jewish forces. Our convoy lay up for a while. We made no attempt to intervene. By this time the indigenous Palestinian Jews had been well organised into a fighting force by the flood of Jewish migrants from continental Europe. The indigenous Arabs were at a great disadvantage. But several escaped German POWs took on the role of officers and tried to organise the Arabs into something of a fighting force. The Jews held the upper hand. Moreover, the Jews were well backed financially and militarily by the United States. The Arabs had no equivalent sponsor. The very next day after our withdrawal, forces from the Arab states surrounding Palestine invaded the country – to no avail. Partition, always a fraught solution, has still to be achieved. It may never be!

*

Soon after my return to Egypt, I was on a troopship heading for England and demobilisation. I was the ship's armoury officer. I shared a cabin with a Captain Quartermaster who rejoiced in the name of *Bottle.* True to his name, Captain Bottle liked a pint or two before lunch. Then, after a good lunch, he repaired to our cabin, stripped down to his string vest and clambered onto his bunk. The beer and the good lunch had their effect. Bottle passed wind, murmuring to himself "Speak up! You're through". Lying on his back when sleep came, Bottle would puff out his lower dentures with every exhalation, neatly sucking them in again with every inhalation. It was as good as a comic opera!

Steaming up the Mersey towards Liverpool, I was overwhelmed by the beauty and greenness of the English countryside compared to the aridity of Egypt. Some years later, as I will recount, I visited Egypt again.

On my return, Moonie and her husband Harold, very kindly put me up in their rather grand flat in Avenue Road, NW8. Harold's widowed and aged father, A.J. Mills was living with them, but there was still a bedroom for me. Old man Mills was a dear. Despite his great wealth, he would say "Malcolm! Let's go on a green line coach to . . . . . I'll pay your fare, but you can pay for our lunch". Harold's elder brother, Frank was by this time the Chairman of *A.J. Mills & Co*. He kindly took us all to the Derby meeting at Epsom. The Queen arrived. The National Anthem was played. I was in uniform, red staff tabs and all. Although I was miles away from the Queen, I saluted. I have never discovered whether that was the correct thing to do.

Immediately after the end of World War II, Moonie arranged for my mother (Jean) and sister (Heather) to emigrate to South Africa and stay in the first instance with Uncle Bertie. Jean would be returning to the land of her birth. Heather‘s employment prospects would probably be better in South Africa than in England. Uncle Bertie was the senior McJannet sibling and a man of standing in East London.

*

My application for an appointment in the Colonial Service (later called the Overseas Civil Service) was under consideration. I was called to an interview conducted by (I imagine) a retired Colonial Servant. He asked "are you going back to Cambridge to complete your degree"? I answered "No! I have to be a wage earner, because I am helping to support my mother." "In that case" he said "I don't think we can offer you an appointment in the Administrative Service. We expect all our young administrative cadets to have university degrees. A degree is like a hallmark on a piece of silver. However, there may be other appointments open to you. Where would you like to serve"? Thinking of my relations in South Africa – Uncle Douglas in Johannesburg and, by that time, Jean and Heather with Uncle Bertie in East London – I said "Basutoland or Swaziland, for preference". He said "These are protectorates, not colonies. By and large, they are administered by peoples appointed by the Government of South Africa".

After a few weeks, I was offered an appointment as a Surveyor in Northern Rhodesia. I accepted immediately. Perhaps my military career had stood me in good stead. Nevertheless I was required to attend a refresher course at the School of Military Survey. "Surveying in the colonies is different from surveying in the army", I was told. One of my instructors at the School of Military Survey turned out to be a Sergeant who had worked for me in the army! How bizarre! But another instructor, Archie

Hamilton had been a surveyor in Northern Rhodesia. So I was able to learn a bit about the country to which I was going, if not much more about surveying,

Northern Rhodesia (now Zambia), I learnt, was a large land-locked country (of nearly 300,000 square miles) in central Africa. It had been administered by Cecil Rhodes's *British South Africa Company* as two separate units (North Western and North Eastern Rhodesia) since the early 1890s, then as a united Northern Rhodesia in 1911. In 1924, the *British South Africa Company*, whilst retaining all the country's mineral rights, handed over the government of Northern Rhodesia to Britain. Britain gave the country protectorate status, unlike its neighbour Southern Rhodesia which was a largely self-governing Crown Colony.

Before the advent of the *British South Africa Company*, there had been a degree of missionary activity in Northern Rhodesia principally by British missionaries, including David Livingstone who had discovered the Victoria Falls in 1855.

I made myself familiar with the lives of Cecil Rhodes and David Livingstone. I armed myself with a valuable book called *Hints to Travellers*. I sailed for Africa on 3 February 1949.

40. OCTU Newark 1948 – Author back row on left, Johnny Watts back row 4th from Left

41. Training as Surveyors 1948 – Author & Andy Heron back row, Johnny Watts front row right

42. Author in dress uniform (later jettisoned in the Mediterranean)

43. Deir Temple Petra – Author in doorway

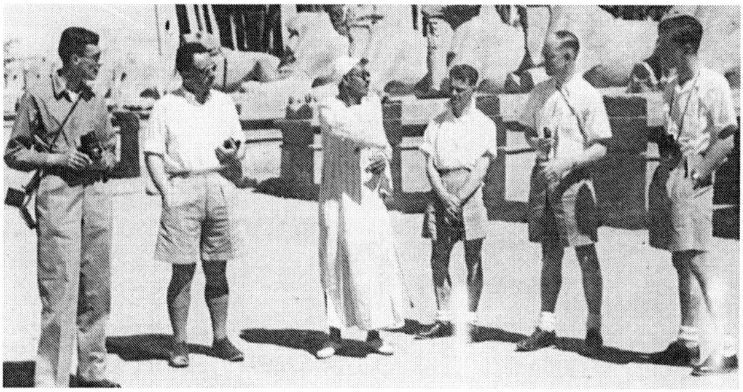

44. In Egypt – author on right next to Lt. Col. Walmesley-White

45. With Rab McEwan in London 1948

Chapter 7

# AFRICA

Travelling to Northern Rhodesia (Zambia) by air was not a valid option in the 1940s. The standard routing was by sea to Cape Town and then by rail, north. It was also possible to travel all the way by road either from South Africa or from Lourenço Marques (now Maputo) in Mozambique. The sea journey to Cape Town took fourteen days: the rail journey from the Cape to Northern Rhodesia's Copperbelt another 4 days of continuous travel. I sailed from Southampton to Cape Town on 3 February 1949, aboard the *Edinburgh Castle.* I shared a cabin with Gordon Cutbush, a member of the Northern Rhodesia Police. Gordon and I soon decided that we would like to get to know two particular girls travelling on our ship: Elizabeth, who was travelling with her parents, and Elsie. We quickly made up a happy foursome. I had hopes that my friendship with Elizabeth would develop into something more intimate and permanent. But it was not to be. At Cape Town, off went Elizabeth with her parents. We lost touch.

When we docked at Cape Town, there was a message from Cousin Gertrude (Gertrude Maskew-Miller – Lalla's cousin) saying that her car and chauffeur were at my disposal for the day. I could be driven around the Cape peninsula, with one or two friends if I wished. On the following day, could I join Cousin Gertrude for lunch at her club? This was a shining example of the wonderful hospitality afforded to all newcomers to South Africa by the European community already established there.

I had already been overwhelmed by the sheer beauty of Table Mountain, clothed in its *tablecloth* of low cloud, as the *Edinburgh Castle* approached Cape Town. Now I was to be equally overwhelmed by the magnificent Cape scenery. Gordon,

Elsie and I were driven off in Cousin Gertrude's car to Constantia Nek, past the University and the Rhodes Memorial. There, at Constantia Neck, we had lunch, before another scenic drive in the afternoon.

The Colonial Office had kindly let me have a few days unpaid leave before I took the train north to Ndola in Northern Rhodesia, so that I could see Jean and Heather who were then living in East London with Uncle Bertie. It was some years since I had last seen them. I remained on the *Edinburgh Castle* until it reached East London. Uncle Bertie had a full house. I therefore put up in a commercial hotel in the city centre. It was basic and rather rough: typical of many commercial hotels in Africa, which I subsequently patronised.

It was, of course, a delight to spend a few days with my family, before heading north by train.

One travelled by South African Railways as far as Bulawayo and then on by Rhodesia Railways (steam trains only in 1949). With luck, there was time to have a bath on the station at Bulawayo, before changing trains. Travel for most Europeans was by first class. Each first class compartment, with its leather-upholstered seats took 4 passengers only (all of the same gender). At night the compartment was converted into 4 bunks. Each bunk was supplied with pillows, sheets and blankets. An attendant (no blacks on South African Railways, no discrimination on Rhodesia Railways) brought you a mug of hot coffee first thing in the morning. There was a very small metal basin, with a trickle of running water, in each compartment and toilet facilities at the end of the corridors in each carriage. There was also a dining car which served reasonable meals. There were blinds and shutters to cover the compartment windows at night, as well as gauzes to keep out insects.

*

When I arrived in Northern Rhodesia in 1949, the protectorate's governance was firmly in the hands of the Colonial Civil Servants, albeit subservient to the British government. The majority of the members of the protectorate's Legislative Council were colonial civil servants: a minority were local inhabitants appointed by the Governor. Gradually more and more members of the Legislative Council were non-officials, at first appointed and later elected under a restricted franchise. In 1953, some powers were transferred from the Northern Rhodesia Government (NRG) to a Federal Government following the establishment of the Central African Federation of Southern Rhodesia (now Zimbabwe), Northern Rhodesia (now Zambia) and Nyasaland (now Malawi). The Federation was highly unpopular with the African inhabitants of Northern Rhodesia and Nyasaland, who were determined to secure self-government. In 1963, the British government disbanded the Federation, Nyasaland and later Northern Rhodesia (in October 1964) were granted their independence. There were elections. The most populous tribe in Northern Rhodesia - the Bemba people – came out on top and ruled the country under the presidency of Kenneth Kaunda. It is no exaggeration to say that members of other African tribes and the European settlers became second class citizens of the independent Zambia.

I took the view that as a civil servant I should stay clear of politics. However, I did get embroiled twice during the ten years of Federation (1953-1962). Towards the end of this period relations between the Federal and Northern Rhodesia Governments became so strained that rumours circulated that the Federal Government intended to enter Northern Rhodesia and arrest the Governor. I became a Special Constable and patrolled the streets of Lusaka (Northern Rhodesia's capital city) nightly. I was still a member of the (British) Regular Army Reserve of Officers. I wrote to the War Office and asked that in the event of conflict in Northern Rhodesia, where should my loyalty lie? The answer was typically evasive!

The second occasion when I became embroiled in politics was in 1962 when the British Government sent a commission out to the Federation, headed by Lord Monckton, to take evidence on the future of the Federation. At that time I was President of the Land Surveyors' Society of Northern Rhodesia. The Society was invited to give evidence. We supported the continuation of the Federation.

For a large country of some 300,000 square miles, Northern Rhodesia was sparsely populated. When I arrived in 1949 there were some 1.6 million Africans, less than 30,000 Europeans and a sprinkling of Asians and people of mixed race. The population grew significantly during the 15 years I lived in Northern Rhodesia. In 1964, when Northern Rhodesia became the independent republic of Zambia, the African population had increased to some 3½ million and the European population to some 75,000. A fair number of the Europeans were not permanent settlers: they were administrators or miners whose intention was to return to Britain or South Africa for their retirement.

*

Arriving by rail in Northern Rhodesia was every bit as dramatic as arriving by sea at Cape Town. A sturdy rail and road bridge spanned the Zambezi River, right beside the mighty Victoria Falls. The train then trundled northwards through predominantly wooded countryside. It stopped at a few small towns en route before reaching Ndola, my destination. There were no platforms at the stations.

If arrival at Ndola was punctual, the driver of the train got a bonus: if arrival was late, the driver got overtime payment. The train had to be very late for the overtime payment to exceed the bonus. It often was! On the Northern Rhodesian section of the line there were no more than 3 trains per week. They carried the mail, as well as passengers.

Ndola was the major town on Northern Rhodesia's Copperbelt and the provincial headquarters of the government (NRG). There was no copper mine at Ndola, but there were 4 major copper mines elsewhere on the Copperbelt. Each mine was served by a virtually autonomous mining settlement twinned with an ordinary town administered by a local authority.

I was met in Ndola by W.M. (Bill) Younger – my boss, the Divisional Surveyor. Bill was a South African who had had a distinguished World War II record, earning him the MBE. He was a chain smoker. Cigarettes were bought in packages containing ten boxes of 50 cigarettes each. Five hundred cigarettes cost less than £1.

Bill Younger drove me to his home where he and his wife, Norah provided me with a bath and a cooked breakfast. (Here was another example of wonderful hospitality)! After breakfast, Bill and I went to the office where I was introduced to the only other land surveyor, Michael Perks. Michael and his family were later to leave Northern Rhodesia for Canada.

The Department of Surveys and Land, my employer, was small. All the land surveyors were British, other than Bill Younger and P. W. M. (Percy) Allin. Much later I came to the conclusion that Percy took rather a dim view of the British land surveyors and that he favoured land surveyors from South Africa, his country of origin. Certainly, by the time that Percy was Surveyor General in the 1960s, there were only four British land surveyors in the government service, in contrast to sixteen South African land surveyors. South African recruitment certainly impeded my career, as will become evident.

Bill Younger gave me Chapter 68 of the Laws of Northern Rhodesia (the Land Survey Ordnance) to study. To my consternation I read that one couldn't practice as a land surveyor in Northern Rhodesia, without a licence. The prerequisites to the grant of a licence were the attainment of a university degree and the passing of a trial survey. Land Surveyors who already had a licence to practice in South Africa could automatically get a Northern Rhodesia licence.

How incongruous! I had been turned down for an appointment in the Colonial Administrative Service because I didn't have a university degree which was **not** obligatory, only to be offered an appointment in the Colonial Survey Service where in order to practice in my profession a degree **was** obligatory.

This was a major setback for me. There was no degree in Land Surveying in Britain. The British-born land surveyors in Northern Rhodesia had geography degrees. It mattered not that my training (and experience) as a land surveyor in the army, far outweighed the amount of land surveying instruction to be had in a geography degree course at a British university.

I then had a stroke of good fortune. The Royal Institution of Chartered Surveyors (RICS) decided to inaugurate a new Land Survey Division. Practising land surveyors with experience (more experience than I then had) were automatically eligible to become Associates of the RICS. I had sufficient qualifications and experience to exempt me from all but the final qualifying examination. I persuaded the Northern Rhodesia Government to amend Chapter 68 of the Laws, so as to recognize Associate Membership of the RICS, in the Land Surveying Division, as an alternative qualification to a geography degree. I set about studying for the final exam, on my own. After a year, I sat the examination in Ndola and passed. I was the first overseas student so to do. The next step was to undertake a trial survey in Northern Rhodesia.

*

A word or two of explanation about land surveying might be helpful. In the army, land surveying could, roughly, be equated with map-making. In other words, it was topographical surveying. In Northern Rhodesia land surveying boiled down to the preparation of dimensioned diagrams of land parcels (whether township plots, smallholdings or farms), for attachment to title deeds. It was cadastral surveying. The basic tools for cadastral surveying were the theodolite for measuring angles, and tapes for measuring distances. There was no means other than tapes for measuring distances in the 1950s. The tapes were of two varieties: an ungraduated 300 foot tape made of invar, a heat-resistant compound metal, and a graduated 100 foot steel tape. Allowances had to be made to compensate for the expansion of the tapes due to high temperatures. The 300 foot tapes were regularly calibrated against fixed markers situated at Livingstone.

When I joined the department it was called the Department of Surveys and Land. In essence, the land comprised only about 6% of the whole of Northern Rhodesia. This was termed *Crown Land.* All the major townships, the copper mines, extensive

Forest Reserves and some large farming areas were situated on Crown Land. Grants of Crown land could be purchased from the government, subject to certain financial qualifications, irrespective of race. In early years, these grants were usually freeholds; later they were leaseholds. Each deed conveying the grant of land had a survey diagram attached to it. The diagram showed the dimensions and the acreage of the land granted and was signed by a licensed land surveyor.. The deed was registered in a Registry housed in the Department of Surveys and Land.

The surveyors who carried out the field work and who prepared the diagrams had to submit all their work to the departmental head office for rigorous examination, before they could sign the diagrams. Sometimes the submission would be returned to the surveyor for (usually minor) alterations to correct any errors that were discovered.

The 94% of Northern Rhodesia which was not Crown Land was set aside for African occupation, under tribal tenure customs. In *Native Reserves* occupation, other than by Africans, was prohibited. In *Native Trust Land* occupation was predominantly for Africans, but mission stations, trading posts or the like could be established with the agreement of a local chief or headman. Anyone could obtain a grant of Crown Land, but economic circumstances and technical competence meant that, in practice, Africans were virtually debarred. Many Africans, of course, left the Reserves and Trust Lands and came for employment to the towns or copper mines situated on Crown Land. They were accommodated in "compounds", which were housing areas sited close to the towns or mines, with limited facilities. Domestic servants were often accommodated in the grounds of their employers. Similarly, Africans who came to work on Crown Land farms would live on those farms as tenants of the farmer. The farm workers were invariably provided with land for growing their own crops: some farmers established schools and clinics on their land, for the use of their labour force.

*

Before I was licensed as a Land Surveyor, Bill Younger had to sign all my surveys as being under his personal supervision. Bill, of course, was a licensed Land Surveyor although, in fact, he had no academic qualification. (Even the law could be ignored)!, One of my first jobs was to assist Bill in a large layout of residential plots at Kitwe, on the Copperbelt. Bill worked on his own on half the layout; similarly I worked on my own on the other half. It was basically a grid layout of plots, the only obstacle to our progress being ubiquitous anthills (in fact made by termites). These anthills could be as great as 15 feet high and 40 feet in circumference at their bases. We got our labourers to cut a two foot wide path through them so that lines of sight and linear measurements were in no way impeded. To cut such a path might take a group of half a dozen labourers as long as two days of gruelling work. Eventually Bill's part of the survey and mine met up in the middle of the layout. There was the minutest discrepancy between the two of us. Thereafter, Bill was happy to sign off any survey work undertaken by me independently, with hardly a check. The four corners of each plot were marked by 6 inch steel pins of about half an inch in diameter, set in concrete.

Some years after my arrival in Ndola, the Government established a town planning department. The town planners frowned on grid layouts of township plots. New layouts incorporated numerous curves, not necessitated by the topography of the site, merely as a design measure. This enormously complicated preliminary calculations and the eventual survey of such layouts. Of course, the actual boundary of any plot could not, in itself, be curvilinear It had to be a straight line arc connecting two points on the curve.

*

My trial survey, the next essential step, after qualifying academically, before getting my licence as a Land Surveyor, was in four parts: a block of smallholdings, a layout of township plots, a block of larger farms and what was termed an astro fix. This latter meant the determination of one's latitude and longitude from observations of the stars at night. Unbeknown to me, I was asked to make an astro fix at a point where the latitude and longitude had already been determined - by no less a person than Percy Allin, then the Deputy Director of Surveys & Land. The inevitable happened: there was a slight discrepancy between our two findings. However, I was able to convince the examiners that my observations couldn't be faulted and that the discrepancy was within the bounds of tolerance. I passed my trial survey and got my licence.

To determine one's latitude and longitude was not such an esoteric exercise as it might first seem. How else was one to determine exactly where one was, in the absence of maps and if the nearest co-ordinated survey point was many miles away? There were, at that time, no topographical maps of Northern Rhodesia, such as the 1/50,000 ordnance survey maps of Great Britain. In any event, the topography comprised an unending expanse of bush country, interspersed by the occasional grassy area (known as dambos) and streams or rivers. A village settlement might be shown on an unreliable sketch map made by a District Officer on tour. He may well have recorded the name of the stream near the village as *katwishi,* having asked a local African for its name and got the reply "katwishi, Bwana" ("I do not know, Sir")! In some parts of the country the village may have moved since the District Officer's visit, because many locals indulged in subsistence farming. This involved cutting the trees down to knee height, burning the felled wood, using the resultant ash as a fertiliser, tilling the ground between the tree stumps and growing sufficient only for the needs of the villagers. When the soil was impoverished, the villagers would move to another area and repeat the process. The villagers might return to the original site in later years, after the trees had grown again.

The railway line was a useful point of reference for a new survey, if it was close enough at hand. The 100 yards wide strip of land reserved for the railway from Livingstone to Ndola had been fully surveyed and beaconed. But the Great North Road, which also ran between Livingstone and Ndola, was useless as a point of reference, away from the few well-spaced settlements along its length. Even after one had become fairly familiar with the road, it was often impossible to know exactly where one was since leaving the last settlement. The mileage travelled was too rough a guide.

A friend went hunting in the bush. (A game licence allowed one to shoot a limited amount of game). He left his vehicle beside the Great North Road and walked off into the bush. By nightfall, he had failed to find his way back to the road. He was unfamiliar with the stars in the southern hemisphere and he had no compass. So he didn't know in which direction he should walk to find the road and his vehicle. Sensibly, he climbed a tree and waited until daybreak. He then knew that he must walk with the sun behind him. He reached the road, but his vehicle was not in sight. Did it lie to the north or to the south? Again sensibly, he didn't start walking in one direction or the other. He waited beside the road - goodness knows for how long – for another vehicle to come. He then flagged it down and asked its driver if he had passed a stationary vehicle and, if so, how far away it was.

*

I shall digress a bit, so as to describe the condition of the roads in Northern Rhodesia in those days. In Livingstone, Lusaka and the towns on the copperbelt, many, but not all of the urban roads had been paved. On the copperbelt, the roads between towns had two paved strips in their centres, just far enough apart to take the tracks of most vehicles. Between these paved strips and on either side of them, the road was unpaved. The practice was to drive in the middle of the road on the two paved strips. If one met a vehicle coming in the opposite direction, both vehicles pulled over to the left. The off-side wheels would then be on one of the paved strips, but the near-side wheels would be in the dirt. This convention would be broken if the Governor or the Provincial Commissioner was travelling with a police escort. One then had to pull over entirely to one's left, leaving both paved strips for the VIP's exclusive use. Since the summer rainfall on the copperbelt was high, one might then get bogged down! By the time I left Northern Rhodesia (1964) all the copperbelt roads were fully paved, as were all the roads in the major townships, but not the Great North Road, the Great East Road and the minor roads serving farming communities.

The Great North and Great East Roads were dirt roads for practically their entire length. They were cambered (to a degree) and graded. It was extremely dusty driving over their impacted earth surface. This surface became very corrugated and one had to maintain a minimum speed in an effort to glide, as it were, from the ridge of one corrugation to the next. The roads were regularly regraded in order to eliminate the corrugations and every so often the road surface would be given a topping of laterite. Despite the heavy summer rains, one seldom got bogged down.

*

The usual practice in our Division at Ndola was to make prior calculations and undertake final drafting work during the wet season. Field work would be concentrated in the dry season. One could practically guarantee that there would be no rain between the beginning of April and mid-October, each year. In October it would become hotter and hotter and thunder clouds would gather until finally the heavens opened. On the copperbelt upwards of 60 inches (1,520 mm.) of rain would then fall over the next 5 or 6 months.

It was also the practice in the Division at Ndola to camp on site when undertaking fieldwork, even if the job was as close as 12 miles from the office. It was sensible, therefore, to complete one's fieldwork (other than perhaps in Ndola itself) during the dry winter months. The first time that I camped "on the job", was for a survey on the Belgian Congo boundary, not many miles from Ndola. It was a novel experience. I had to make adequate provision for my labour force, for my vehicle and for myself, in the knowledge that eyebrows would be raised, at the very least, should I find it necessary to return to Ndola for any oversight in provisions. I immediately learnt not to drop my dirty stockings on the floor of my tent. On my first night in camp, they had provided a tasty meal for the ubiquitous ants!

My labour force was under the supervision of an African Assistant Surveyor, who had received a measure of training as a surveyor at a Departmental Training School. He was assisted by an African Chainman, more often than not an experienced and intelligent labourer who had been promoted. I took with me my own personal African servant. Shortly after we had established camp, my servant brought an attractive young African woman to my tent. Clearly, she was offering her services as my concubine! She got short shrift, but a tot of methylated spirits when she asked for a drink of spirits. She downed this with gusto! I was never troubled in the same way subsequently.

At night fall, shortly after 6 p.m., I would light my tent with a Tilley Lamp (hence the methylated spirits) and a couple of hurricane lamps. The Africans would make themselves a good fire, using the plentiful amount of firewood always at hand. I used to take a galvanised iron hip bath whenever I went camping. Small drums of water would be heated up over the camp fire so that I could have a reasonably hot bath before my evening meal. In all my years of camping, I never once missed my evening dip. I made sure that we always camped near a source of water.

*

I had learnt to drive when I was in the army. I had a driving licence, but no car of my own. A new Ford *Cortina* cost £600. My annual salary was £550 for the first two years, then £620, rising by annual increments of £35 to £1,320. A new car was out of the question. Fortunately, the office had several government-owned vehicles: a couple of Chevrolet pick-up trucks, a 5-ton lorry and a small jeep-like car. It was accepted practice to make use of an office vehicle for journeys between home and office

I was aged about 30 when I got my first vehicle. It was a second-hand Austin van. It gave me trouble and I got rid of it as soon as I could afford a new car. It became my custom to pick up a new car at Southampton docks, when I arrived there on long leave (a period of 6 months every two and a half years) on a *Union Castle* liner. I made something of a gaffe the first time I did this. I got a taxi from the ship to the car dealers. My bags were deposited on the pavement. I went into the salesroom, announced who I was and asked if someone would collect my bags. Frozen looks! I was no longer in Africa where there were always willing hands to help out, however trivial the chore. There were considerable tax savings in collecting a car in England, provided it was exported within 6 months. These advantages outweighed the costs of shipping the car back to Africa. In Africa no duty was demanded.

I came home from the office, one evening, in the jeep-like office car and parked it outside my house. Next morning I found a lady's handbag on the passenger seat. I rang the girl to whom I had given a lift, but she said the bag wasn't hers. I then looked inside it. I found a bill with a name on it. I knew the person in question was the girlfriend of my neighbour. How her handbag had got into the car during the night remained a matter for conjecture! I wrapped the bag up in a parcel, addressed to the owner, and asked an African Orderly to deliver it to her personally, at her office. When the Orderly returned, I asked him if he had done what I had asked. He replied "I gave it to the Bwana, Sir". Horror of horrors! The woman's husband – the "Bwana" – worked in the same office as his wife. Nothing more was heard by me!

On another occasion, I had returned home in the office 5-ton truck. My neighbour at that time was a policeman called Hookham. (He was a cousin of Margot Fonteyn). Hookham said "are you licensed to drive a 5-ton vehicle"? I wasn't. Hookham said "bring your licence to the police station and I will endorse it for you". Next day I drove the truck to the police station. The licence was endorsed. As I drove away, I knocked down a boundary post! Nothing was said!

The Commissioner of Police was Colonel J.P.I. Fforde. His (second) wife had a title in her own right. She was Lady Jean Fforde, a daughter of the 6th Duke of Montrose. Hookham told me that he had seen the Colonel's passport. After his surname of Fforde there was written in brackets *formerly Ford.* Clearly, if you have a titled wife, the surname of plain *Ford* rather lets the side down!

A more dramatic driving incident happened when I was stationed at Livingstone. I was then living in a government hostel where most of the other residents were young girls. One girl, who had the use of an open-back pick-up truck, but only a provisional driving licence, asked me if I would go with her and some of her friends to the Victoria Falls Hotel, where they wanted to have a swim. Off we set, the girl driving, I sitting beside her in the front and 5 or 6 more girls sitting in the back. After ten minutes or so, I smelt burning. I asked the driver to stop. I got out. It was evident that the brakes were binding. I told the driver to take the truck to a garage next day and have the brakes tested. She said she had only just got the truck back after a full service. We drove on. The burning smell persisted. Just before we got to the road/rail bridge spanning the Zambezi River, I asked the girl to draw in to the side. The girls piled out of the back of the truck to view the Falls. I said "I really think we should go no further. I will turn the vehicle round, let the brakes cool down and then **I** will drive it back to Livingstone". I reversed into the lay-by and applied the foot brake. Nothing happened. I quickly pulled on the hand brake. Still the truck moved backwards. I managed to jump out as it gracefully toppled down an embankment onto the railway line. It came to rest on its side, plumb in the centre of the track! I quickly switched off the engine.

It was essential to alert the authorities as quickly as possible. There were no mobile phones in those days, so one girl was told to flag down the first car and ask its driver to get in touch with the police. Another girl was sent up the railway track to flag down any approaching train, by waving her bathing towel. Similarly a third girl went in the opposite direction, for the same purpose. Most fortunately a break-down vehicle arrived and lifted the truck off the railway tracks before there was any train. We hitched our way back to Livingstone.

A few days later, I was summonsed by the police to appear in court on a charge of dangerous driving. The police also wrote to the Survey Department, requesting a plan of the scene of the accident. Since I was the only qualified land surveyor in Livingstone at the time, I prepared and signed the plan.

When the case came to court, the magistrate immediately said "is that your signature on the bottom of the plan given to me by the police"? "Yes, Sir", I said. "But you can't lead evidence against yourself"! "I have no objection to the plan being used", I replied.

The garage that had recovered the truck gave evidence that the brakes were in perfect working order when they got the vehicle back to their workshops. I had my witnesses about the brakes binding just before the accident. I also established the fact that the garage which had recovered the truck was the very garage which had given the vehicle a clean bill of health the day before the accident.

The magistrate asked us all to accompany him to the scene of the accident. By this time the truck was roadworthy once more. It was used to take some of the witnesses. I wasn't driving it! When we reached the scene of the accident and the magistrate had had a good look round, he asked me to get into the truck and demonstrate just what I had intended to do, before the accident occurred. A cordon of police lined the edge of the embankment! I backed the truck, applied the brakes and then moved forward, with no difficulty. "Case dismissed" said the magistrate! The incident of break failure was a recurring theme in my dreams for many years.

Another scare involving car travel happened when I was driving my own car, at night, from Salisbury (now Harare) to Lusaka. It is a twisting road down the escarpment until one reaches the floor of the Zambezi valley. One has to drive slowly. Then, once on the straight road across the valley, one can put one's foot down on the accelerator and belt away. There was no 70 m.p.h. limit on Rhodesian roads. Suddenly I saw two elephants immediately ahead, standing on my side of the road. (I have a theory that elephants favour coming onto the highway at night. It is more comfortable for them to defecate there, than in the bush). Fortunately for me, I just had sufficient time to swerve round them and avoid them. One touch would have resulted in a nasty accident. My heart was in my mouth!

46. Voyage to Africa 1949 – with Elizabeth

47. Voyage to Africa 1949 – with Gordon Cutbush and Elizabeth

48. Arrival Cape Town – Table Mountain

49. Arrival Northern Rhodesia – Victoria Falls

Chapter 8

# STILL IN AFRICA

Let me go back to Ndola and my first tour of duty (1949-1952). Soon we had three more land surveyors in the office; two licensed surveyors from South Africa and one young Englishman with a Cambridge degree. Because of their qualifications, they were all, in effect, senior to me. But I had to show them the ropes. I suffered in silence! I recalled sadly that I hadn't returned to Cambridge to get my degree.

It was a fact that all the officers in the Administrative Branch were graduates. By and large, they were intelligent and competent, although inclined to assume airs and graces. My boss, Bill Younger was a down-to-earth South African. An administrative officer asked him, at a dinner party, whether he had been to Oxford or to Cambridge. "To Oxford", he replied. "Oh! And to which college"? "To most of them", Bill said, "on a sightseeing tour".

The P.A. (Provincial Administration) as we called the administrative officers sometimes sought aggrandisement by falsely double-barrelling their surnames. M.M. Heggs was put out if one didn't call him Maurice Mitchell-Heggs. Little did he know that the Africans called him *'am-an'-eggs*! A local solicitor called Smith became *Richmond-Smith.* When I was introduced to him, I couldn't refrain from saying, rudely, "how interesting. I have heard of Richmond, Surrey and of Richmond, Yorkshire, but never before of Richmond-Smith"!

Early in 1949, I shared a house with a middle-ranking member of the P.A. called Nicholas Charles Algernon Ridley. There was no need for him to assume a double-barrel with such a splendid string of names! Nick Ridley was a bachelor. He rang the Secretariat in Lusaka saying that he would like to entertain two female secretaries one weekend. Elaborate preparations were made for their reception: special menus, flowers, boxes of chocolates in their bedrooms and so forth. Nick subsequently married one of them (Dorothy Dunlop). I believe it was a very successful and fruitful match. Perhaps I should have taken a lesson from his book! Nick eventually became the Permanent Secretary of the Ministry of Transport and Works.

Nick was also instrumental in establishing the first exclusively black African township on Crown Land. It was called *Twapia.* I laid out the plots, as a weekend job. Twapia was a prototype for more black African townships on Crown Land.

The Deputy Provincial Commissioner at Ndola was called Gervas Clay. He had been a Cambridge Blue. His wife, Betty, was the daughter of Baden-Powell. Gervas carpeted me one day for splashing mud onto the legs of his secretary as she walked to the office and I was driving one of our trucks on an unpaved road. I apologised, of course, and said I would pay for any necessary washing or cleaning. But Gervas refused to acknowledge that it was virtually impossible to drive on a dirt surface, after heavy rain, however slowly, without some mud splashing up.

Later in his career, Gervas became the Provincial Commissioner in the Southern Province. One of his District Commissioners in the Province was a delightful, eccentric, well-heeled man called Mickey Chittenden. (Mickey had his tea supplies flown out from Fortnum and Mason, in London)! It was etiquette for a Provincial Commissioner to advise his District Commissioners if he was travelling in their districts in an official capacity. Gervas neglected so to advise Mickey. To compound this breach of courtesy, Gervas wrote to Mickey criticising something or other which he (Gervas) had spotted. Mickey replied "if I knew you were coming, Sir, I would have baked a cake"!

The wife of a Provincial Commissioner in the Eastern Province, who shall remain nameless, was rather too conscious of her husband's status. She decided that their house should be redecorated and she called in the P.W.D. (Public Works Department). A lowly official arrived and was taken round the house "I want this room decorated in primrose yellow . . . this room decorated in eau de nil . . . this room decorated in duck egg blue . . . ." Eventually the grande dame realised that the lowly official from the P.W.D. was taking no notes, nor making any comment. "Is that quite clear" she asked? "Madam", he replied, "buff is the colour in the P.W.D. and buff you'll bloody well get"! It should be said that the P.W.D. was sometimes called *Perhaps We Do, Perhaps We Don't*!

*

The Government provided officers with housing, including basic items of furniture, such as tables, chairs and beds. However, there was often a shortage of housing. A consequence was that one couldn't retain one's house when away on long leave. All one's goods had to be packed up and put in a government store. The house might then be allocated to another officer for six months. There was no guarantee that one got the same house back after returning from long leave.

The house I finally lived in was at 35 Birch Road, Lusaka. Residential properties were not numbered: instead a small wooden board was planted at the entrance to the property on which one's name was inscribed – M.I.D. Sutherland.

Reverting to early days in Ndola, after living for a short while with Nick Ridley, I shared a house with an Ulsterman, J.A. (Paddy) White. He became a life-long friend. Paddy was married and had two young children, but he had left his family behind in Northern Ireland. Paddy was a Livestock Officer, in essence an unqualified vet. His duties entailed much travelling. He never knew just when he would get back to our house but his African servant whom he had left behind was usually able to say, with accuracy, "Bwana White will be returning home tomorrow". Was it telepathy, or was it a message conveyed across the bush by drums?

On an occasion when Paddy was away on tour, I noticed that our whisky was disappearing, although I was not touching it. I marked the level of the whisky on the label on the bottle and a few days later saw that the level had dropped. I summoned our servants and accused them of theft, which they strongly denied. I then showed them my evidence. Their response was "if we had known you had marked the label, the whisky would not have been stolen". Clearly, **I** was at fault, not them!

Paddy told me that he was so proud to be appointed to the Colonial Service that he arrived by train at Ndola at 6 a.m., wearing a black Homburg hat! That must have caused a lot of amusement. Paddy always wore a tie, however hot it was. (It was not until my final years of service that a standard form of attire seemed to be obligatory for officers in Lusaka. This consisted of open-neck white shirt, white shorts, white stockings and white or black shoes).

Paddy was determined that I should marry, or at least have a steady girl friend. He lined up one attractive girl after another, but I was not hooked. The Foster family had three attractive daughters. I believe the middle girl was in love with me, but I fancied the youngest. She, sadly, wasn't interested!

While on the subject of girls, I might mention the young pretty daughters of two doctors in Ndola – Doctors Acheson and Gilbert. Shortly after my arrival, the two mothers gave a joint party for their daughters. I was invited. Was it because I was still shy with girls, or was it because I found most of the guests to be young teenagers? Whatever the reason, I didn't mingle as much as I should have done. Dear Mrs Gilbert noticed my reticence and quickly invited me to join the few parents for a glass of whisky. Dr. Gilbert had lost the use of his right arm, but it didn't prevent his being a good amateur golfer. The only concession was that he played off the ladies' tees.

*

My sister got married in Johannesburg in 1951. Jean had been living with her up until then. Paddy told me that it was now my duty to provide a home for her. He was right. Paddy and I therefore parted and I was allocated a one-bedroom semi-detached cottage. Jean joined me and had the bedroom. I slept on a camp bed in the living room. Paddy gave us a Jack Russell terrier (not quite a pedigree dog!) called *Punch*. We kept Punch until the day I left Northern Rhodesia. He was a wonderful companion and a good watch dog. I was relieved that he was with Jean, when I went off camping.

Paddy's wife, Dorothy arrived, with their two children. Dorothy was kindness itself both to Jean and to me. Her son, Ronnie became a great friend of Jean. When, some years later, we lived in Lusaka and Ronnie was at boarding school there, he came regularly to have Sunday lunch with us, followed by a walk with Punch and me. (Paddy and Dorothy, at this time, were stationed at Mazabuka – too far away for Ronnie to make a Sunday visit).

Stephen Dunk, a divorcé was a neighbour in Ndola. Before Jean arrived, he made a habit of dropping in and relating from end to end the book that he had just read. It made no difference if I said "Stephen, I am going to bed now". He would follow me into the bathroom and then into the bedroom and sit on the end of the bed until the story was finally finished. Only then did he go home. Stephen was kind to Jean, when she arrived. He remarried a charming French woman. When he retired, they settled in France, but Stephen didn't live long thereafter.

Another kind friend and neighbour in Ndola was A.W. (Alf) Hunter, a bachelor schoolmaster. We kept in touch with him for many years after his retirement to Grayshott in Surrey. He called his house there *Kariba* after the Kariba Dam on the Zambezi River.

A missionary couple with the surname Thomas lived in the cottage behind ours. A baby was born. Jean asked "what are you going to call him"? With a straight face, the missionary's wife said "John William. You see there are so many **John Thomases** around already". Jean found it hard not to laugh! When I told Bill Younger this story, he capped it. When he was staying in a hotel on his honeymoon, he asked his newly-wed bride what she would like to drink before dinner. Norah thought it would be rather sophisticated to ask for a *John Collins*. She turned to the waiter and said "could I have a **John Thomas**, please"?!

Paddy and I occasionally had a round of golf. I continued to be hopeless at the game and soon realised that no amount of practice or coaching was going to turn me into a reasonable golfer. Michael Perks, from the office, was an excellent golfer. Once, he spent rather a long time addressing the ball. A swarm of ants climbed up his stockinged legs and under his shorts before he realised what was happening. When the ants reached a certain delicate part of his anatomy, one of them must have given the order "all bite now"! It was excruciating. Poor Michael flung down his club, jumped into the bushes, pulled down his shorts and got rid of the mischief makers.

After Michael told me this story, I instructed the African who held an umbrella over my instrument in the field (to shield it from the sun), when I was making my observations, to watch out for ants. If an ant ever got above the top of one of my stockings, the African would be in dire trouble. A certain amount of gentle swatting sometimes went on, as I peered into my theodolite or level, but no ant ever progressed above the top of my stockings!

*

Ants came in many varieties and were a curse. Instead of **damp**-proof courses, houses were built with **ant**-proof courses – thin sheets of metal protruding beyond one of the brick courses near ground level. In theory, ants could not negotiate this obstacle and get into the house. Nevertheless, ants would find their way into one's house now and again. They usually made for the kitchen, where crumbs might be found. The legs of one's meat-safe would be placed in small tins of water; another effective obstacle for the ants. There was a tale of a colony of ants attacking a chicken penned in a coop, over night. Next morning, all that was left in the coop were the chicken's feathers and bones.

Mosquitoes were also prevalent in Northern Rhodesia. Malaria was rife. One took prophylactics regularly. I was already aware of the danger of catching malaria. When I was in the army, stationed in Egypt, an Order came: "From [date], long trousers will be worn and sleeves will be rolled down after sunset".

Had the mosquitoes been told that they mustn't bite before the proscribed date?!

The windows of our houses in Northern Rhodesia were protected by fly screens, to keep out all flying insects, including mosquitoes. Nevertheless at certain times of the year – and always in camp – it was advisable to sleep under a mosquito net. The method of determining whether one had contracted malaria was by the examination of a blood slide. This task (I was in Ndola at the time) was performed by an African medical orderly. He once failed to detect, from a blood slide, that the patient did, in fact, have malaria. He was reprimanded. Africans, one soon discovered, always wanted to please, irrespective of the truth. They would cheerfully tell a lie, if they thought that that was the answer which would best please the inquirer. The African medical orderly who had been reprimanded was upset because, clearly, he hadn't pleased the doctor. It was believed that from then on, this particular orderly said that every slide which he examined showed signs of malaria. Surely that was what the doctor wanted to hear.

Whether or not it was a faulty diagnosis when a blood slide was taken from me, it was said that the blood sample showed that I had malaria. I thought that all I was suffering from was a bad bout of influenza. A cure for malaria was prescribed. I felt much worse. I threw the remaining pills away and recovered. I have never had a recurrence of fever, if indeed it was malaria in the first instance. After I had retired and had returned to England the Blood Transfusion Service was quite happy to take blood donations from me, despite my medical history.

*

When I arrived in Northern Rhodesia, the Director of Surveys and Land was S.F. (Sammy) Turner. The Deputy Director was R.M. (Solly) Garrard.

Sammy Turner's wife was far from well. Sammy consoled himself with the Departmental Secretary, Theo Hockey – a widow. This gave rise to the quip "he is only the Director of Surveys, but he knows how to give his Theo delight (theodolite)".

Sammy's wife died. He then married Theo.

Solly Garrard moved to Nyasaland (now Malawi) to become the Director of Surveys in that colony. I had never met him, but a few years after his move to Nyasaland he invited me to apply for the number three post in his Department, with the prospect of soon becoming the Deputy Director. I suspect that Solly had had a favourable account of me from Bill Younger, assuredly not from P.W.M. (Percy) Allin, who had become Deputy Director of Surveys and Land in Northern Rhodesia, after Solly's departure.

As already mentioned, I had gained the impression that Percy Allin thought that the British surveyors (of whom I was one, of course) were a pretty poor lot, compared to the South African surveyors. Until much later, after Percy had become the Surveyor General (a post replacing that of Director of Surveys and Land) and I had risen a few notches, it seemed to me that Percy was always having a go at me. Percy gave me a particularly tough assignment in 1953, hoping I suspect, to get me out of his way, for a while. I shall write about this later. After I had become the Divisional Surveyor at Choma in the Southern Province, Percy snapped at me when I asked for necessary stationery and drafting equipment for my office. "Get out into the field and do some fieldwork", he said. When I was surveying a large block of farms some 15 miles south of Choma, Percy complained because I struck camp every Friday evening and returned to Choma until Sunday evening. This, he no doubt thought, was the sloppy behaviour of an effete Englishman. I had to point out that I was the only surveyor at Choma, that I had no secretary and that I had to run the office as part of my duty. If he thought I was slacking, I hope he took note that in successive Departmental Annual Reports, the Choma Division topped the league table of work completed, when I was the Divisional Surveyor there.

I must say it rankled with me that the increasing number of licensed land surveyors from South Africa earned more than me and were regarded as senior to me, despite the fact that I had been appointed before them. The trouble was that for several years I was unqualified in the eyes of the law (as well as being considered inferior by Percy, I am sure). D.J.B. (Dudley) Copeland was the first of the post-war South African appointees. I had to show him the ropes in Ndola and I regarded myself every bit as, if not more competent than he. This “gap” between us came to a head in 1964. Dudley was then the Deputy Surveyor General. I was the Deputy Director of Lands. When the post of Surveyor General became vacant, we both applied for it. Dudley got the appointment.

Earlier, my frustration at being leap-frogged and my seeming lack of favour in the eyes of Percy Allin reached the ears of Aunt Moonie in England. Her husband Harold (Mills) most generously offered to finance my setting up as a surveyor in private practice, should I decide to resign from the Government service. But I soldiered on. I cherished the security of being on the permanent staff, in the Colonial Survey Service.

*

I returned to Africa from long leave for my second tour of duty towards the end of 1952. There was a cable for me at Cape Town which said “Do not return to Ndola. Report for duty at Livingstone”. Fortunately, I was on my own. Jean had remained in England with Heather and didn’t rejoin me until after I had been posted to Choma. All my goods and chattels were in store in Ndola, but there was no point in moving them south until I knew how long I was likely to be stationed in Livingstone. I found accommodation in the government hostel there.

Livingstone had been the capital of Northern Rhodesia, but it was poorly located for the seat of government. It was decided to remove the capital to Lusaka, which was in a central situation. The Director of Surveys and Land and some senior staff had relocated to Lusaka, but all the departmental draughtsmen and survey examiners had remained in Livingstone. I was instructed to help clean up the back log of surveys which had been lodged for examination. I was not too happy if I found an error and was obliged to return the work to the surveyor who had undertaken the survey, for corrections to be made.

It was high summer (mid-winter in England). Livingstone was as hot as hell. I would rise from a sleepless night at 5 a.m., have a cold shower, but find I was perspiring freely again by 6 a.m.

Most of the residents at the government hostel in Livingstone were girls. I fell in love with one of them, an attractive South African girl called Pam Richards. But it came to nothing, I fear. First, it was not long before I had to leave Livingstone. I had cleared up the backlog of examination work. Secondly, I was providing a home for my mother. I couldn't afford to run two homes. What girl would want to share a house with her mother-in-law? Shortly after leaving Livingstone, I sent Pam some handkerchiefs with the message:

Too late for tears, it appears.
But does a modern miss use
Only tissues?

In retrospect, I wonder if my love of Pam was as profound as it seemed at the time. Certainly, I didn't pop the question. I would probably have been rejected in any event. I confess, too, that I was not averse, at the same time, to having mild flirtations with the wives of two of our draughtsmen! Was I a libertine? Was it all a side effect of the hot weather?

*

The Victoria Falls, on the doorstep of Livingstone, are reduced almost to a trickle before the rains break and the Zambezi River flows strongly once more. Some daring people (not me) would hop from rock to rock at the summit of the Falls, when the river was at its lowest, traversing from one bank to the other. The surrounding area of the Falls was completely unspoilt. The only development was the road and rail bridge over the river. In 1964, an American entrepreneur wanted to build a luxury hotel within sight of the Falls. I was much against this idea, but my boss, the Commissioner of Lands Sydney Burlock, favoured it. Today, sadly, the Falls are scarred by development.

*

I have already mentioned that I was once given a "tough

assignment" by Percy Allin. This occurred after I had left Livingstone in 1953. My task was to take observations at a chain of primary triangulation stations located between Lusaka and Fort Jameson (now Chipata), on behalf of the Directorate of Colonial Surveys. This chain of triangulation stations had been established some years previously, but no observations had been taken. Some of the wooden beacons which had been built over these triangulation stations were still extant. Others had been lost or were damaged and had to be replaced or restored. It was, of course, an immense advantage to have an earlier reconnaissance survey to develop, whether or not some of the original beacons had to be rebuilt or renovated. Another major advantage was that the chain of triangulation stations lay on either side of the Great East Road which connected Lusaka to Fort Jameson.

A base (one side of a triangle) had to be measured at the Lusaka end of the chain. The site for this base had already been chosen. The measurements, taken three times to ensure accuracy to a decimal point of an inch, presented no difficulty. Then theodolite observations had to be taken at every (restored) triangulation station in the chain. These stations were on hill tops, perhaps as far as 15 miles into the bush, either side of the Great East Road. The distance between adjacent triangulation stations could be 30 miles or more. Because of the heat haze, observations could be made only very early in the morning or late in the afternoon. The result was that I might have to spend two or more days at any particular triangulation station in order to complete my observations.

I established a base camp on the Great East Road about halfway between Lusaka and Fort Jameson and used my 3-ton lorry to transport my labour force, equipment and temporary camping gear up and down that road to a point nearest to the triangulation station to be visited. No such station was more than a two days trek through the bush, from the Great East Road. Everything had to be carried on these treks through the bush. For this purpose, I employed a labour force of 30 or 40 men. Their food had to be carried too, of course, because there were very few villages where food might be purchased.

The labourers were simple peasant people, living in the area. Word had soon got round – as it always does in Africa – that I was on my way, so I had no difficulty in recruiting sufficient numbers. Some of the men had been involved in the earlier reconnaissance survey. This was a great help in finding a suitable route through the bush from the Great East Road to a triangulation station. Each trek was through typical bush country, with no roads or tracks and limited long- range visibility. On several occasions, I had to get one of my men to climb a tree to look for the next triangulation station and then point us in the requisite direction. The strength and endurance of the labourers were remarkable. Each man had to carry a load weighing up to 50 pounds. True, they would drag their heels a bit on an outward journey from my truck on the Great East Road, but once the observations had been completed and the beacon rebuilt, they would walk me off my feet on the return journey to my lorry.

I had to be completely self-sufficient. There was no means of communicating with the outside world, but I did have a small portable radio. To hear a man's voice speaking on the radio left many of the labourers completely awe-struck. I carried a rifle (or, rather, asked my headman to carry my rifle), but during the two and a half months that the exercise lasted, no game was shot for the pot. None was found. Even when I could let the headman take a day off to go hunting, he would return empty handed. If we passed a village, I would try to buy a chicken or two. Once we had a real treat when I was able to buy a small pig.

One particular incident is worth recording. My labourers wanted to stop and pitch camp rather early one afternoon, when we came across a village by a small stream. I insisted that we should push on for another two hours, because I knew the following day's trek would be long enough. After we had completed the extra two hours journey and halted for the night, one or two labourers asked for permission to return to the village. I readily gave permission. The only condition was that they should be back and ready to move at daybreak the next day. A roll-call was taken at daybreak. One labourer was missing. Another had a bout of fever. I sent the latter man back to the village with his and the missing man's kit. I told him that both of them should await my return in two or three days' time. When I got back to the village, the labourer with fever had recovered, but the other man was still missing. I spoke to the village headman. He told me that some of the villagers had scoured the neighbouring bush, but they had found no trace of the missing man. When I returned to civilisation (i.e. to Lusaka), I reported the incident to the police, to whom I gave the missing man's kit. No inquest was held. No questions were asked. It was simply assumed that the man had lost his way in the dark when returning from the village to my camp, and that he had been taken by a lion. His kit was sent to his home village.

The whole exercise took me two and a half months. I estimated that I had walked 430 miles. I certainly knew that I had established camp in 41 different locations. I think Percy Allin hoped he was keeping me quiet for six months, or more!

*

Home leave was generous: 6 months after a tour of 2 years and a half. One received full pay on leave and all one's travelling expenses were paid. Provided one travelled to a temperate destination, the passage money could be used for travel other than to Britain – to the United States, say. The South African surveyors enjoyed this privilege (passage money to Britain) as well as the British surveyors. People like Dudley Copeland and his wife, Barbara were able to visit Europe for the first time, at government expense. We could also take "local" leave of up to 14 days each year. I never took more than a day or two. In retrospect, that was a mistake. I should have taken the opportunity to see far more of Northern Rhodesia, outside the Crown Land areas.

When going on long leave, I liked to travel by rail to Cape Town and then by sea to Britain. I was told that the firm who had built part of the South African track, north of Cape Town, were paid on a mileage basis. Because of this, so it was said, the track followed a very circuitous route in hilly areas, despite the fact that a less tortuous route with rather steeper gradients was quite feasible. Be that as it may, one could frequently look out of the window in a leading carriage and see the tail end of the train. The construction of the track in Northern Rhodesia was partly paid for by the grant of freehold farms measuring one mile by one mile, strung out on either side of the track. These farms were virtually valueless, either through lack of water or through poor soil conditions.

On one occasion travelling by train south to Cape Town, there had been heavy rains in the area of Beaufort West. The track was damaged. Major repairs were necessary and all the trains arriving at Beaufort West were held up there. Eventually, there were three trains there: the train from Bulawayo (my train), which had arrived first; then the Orange Express and finally the Blue Train from Johannesburg. The Blue Train is South Africa's finest: the Orange Express is not far behind in excellence. So it was no surprise that, after the track had been repaired, the trains departed in the reverse order of their arrival!

I was exercising my legs on the platform of Beaufort West, when a passenger from one of the South African trains addressed me in Afrikaans. "I am sorry, Sir", I said, "but I don't speak Afrikaans". He promptly turned on his heels and walked away. I mention this because it exemplifies the deep-seated antipathy between the Afrikaners and the South Africans of British descent. It was as if the Boer War had happened only yesterday.

Northern Rhodesia was less bedevilled by racial divisions than was South Africa. There was no policy of apartheid separating whites, coloured and blacks. Nevertheless, it was not an integrated society in Northern Rhodesia. Language and culture tended even to separate the Afrikaners who had moved up from South Africa, from other white inhabitants. Massive economic differences between whites and blacks reinforced the divisions created by language and culture.

As well as paying one's African servants a basic wage (abysmally small in comparison to one's own income), it was customary to give them a small allowance for the purchase of basic food. I am ashamed to say that I spent nearly as much on feeding my dog, as I did on the allowance for each servant's food. When the government proposed a statutory increase in the wages paid to the orderlies and labourers in their employ, I argued (to my shame) that wages should be determined solely by economic factors.

*

Reverting to my overseas leaves, sailing to and from Cape Town on the ocean wave seemed to be conducive to romance. I have already mentioned my first (adult) love for Elizabeth, on my first trip to Africa. On a subsequent Africa-bound voyage, I fell for an attractive young woman called Sheila. The snag was that Sheila was already married and she had a young child. That didn't seem to deter either of us. Sheila's husband was a fellow passenger, and a fellow officer in Northern Rhodesia. Jean (my mother) was also a passenger. They both probably viewed what was going on with some concern, but nothing was said – at least to me. When we got back to Northern Rhodesia, Sheila and her husband were posted to Livingstone: I to Choma. Livingstone and Choma were far enough apart for the flame to dwindle. That was really a blessing.

It became increasingly viable and popular to fly home on leave. Jean and I made one trip by air, stopping off en route at Nairobi, Athens, Zurich, Rome and Paris. At Zurich airport we were met by the hotel's (*Baur au Lac*) vintage Rolls Royce. The hotel restaurant was most expensive. I noticed one guest making a meal of repeated helpings of hors d'oeuvre – nothing else! In that way he saved quite a lot of money! In Rome, I threw my small Greek coins, which I had picked up in Athens, into the Trevi Fountain. This was meant to ensure a subsequent visit to Rome. The coins floated in the water! They were made of papier mâché. But I did return to Rome much later.

I think it was at the end of this particular leave that I returned to Africa by way of car to Trieste, then by *Shaw Saville* line from Trieste to Lourenço Marques (Maputo) and finally by car again to Lusaka. My brother-in-law, Hardy accompanied me on the first leg of the journey. We motored to Lydd (in Kent), drove the car onto a plane and took off for Le Touquet. We had one or two night stops before reaching the Riviera, where Hardy unexpectedly left me and flew back to England. There was no quarrel: was he just bored? While we were in Paris, a motor cavalcade passed down the Champs Elysée. Eisenhower was on a state visit. Beside him, in his open car, sat De Gaulle. At a halt in Switzerland, I was roundly berated by a shopkeeper for sampling a grape before buying the bunch. On the Riviera, after Hardy's departure, I got thoroughly lost trying to find a post office. I wanted to buy stamps and post some postcards. I eventually found a post office, after asking for directions three times. The stamps were purchased, the cards were posted. But where had I parked my car? The car was laden with all my goods, including my passport and my traveller's cheques. I had to walk up and down half a dozen streets systematically, before I eventually found the car. Oh, what a relief! On my way through Italy, I tried to find the villa near Lonigo which had been the officers' mess when I was serving with 19 Field Survey Company. No success!

I disembarked at Port Said and took a taxi to Cairo, so as to revisit the Pyramids and the wonderful Cairo museum. The taxi driver nearly lynched me when I told him that I could see no discernible changes following Nasser's succession to power! I rejoined the ship at Suez. The ship didn't anchor there. A launch took me alongside, and I transferred from one vessel to the other while they were both moving.

I shared a cabin with a bright young teenager who was travelling back to South Africa with his father (a Doctor), mother and sister. Inevitably, I fell for the sister, Elsie. I am confident that my feelings for Elsie were reciprocated. After we went our separate ways on reaching Africa, we corresponded for a time and the good Doctor and his wife called on me in my office in Lusaka, a few weeks later. I cannot remember what brought our romance to an end. It was probably a case of absence **not** making the heart grow fonder. In retrospect, perhaps I was not fully committed to Elsie. Why else would I have found her shipboard girlfriend equally attractive?

*

On one of my home leaves, Jean and I drove to Newcastle-on-Tyne and took the car ferry to Bergen. En route, we stopped at Hull, to meet Uncle Bertie's son Ian with his fiancée, Gill. When my brand new car was off-loaded at Bergen, there was a large gash the length of the off-side. The car had not been stowed securely. Fortunately, it was still roadworthy. Eventually the shipping company paid for the repairs.

I bought a good wristwatch in Bergen, where there was no duty on such goods. The watch stopped a day or two after we had left the town I rang the jewellers. Nobly, they had a brand new replacement watch ready for me when we got back to Bergen.

We had a planned itinerary in Norway. We went from one excellent and hospitable hotel to another, enjoying the spectacular scenery on the way. In one hotel I admired a porcelain ashtray in the lounge, which had been made by a local potter. Immediately, I was given one to take away with me. Such was the hospitality of the Norwegians.

At the country hotels, the custom at dinner was that all the guests should be seated before the meal was served. The waitresses lined up against the walls, facing the diners. Once everyone was seated, the first course would be served. Sometimes there would be a pianist playing – inevitably music by Grieg.

The country hotels were of wood construction. Any fire, of course, could spread rapidly. To allow for that eventuality, each bedroom had its own fire escape – a rope ladder which could be attached to the window sill and rolled down to ground level.

We adored Norway; not only the wonderful scenery, but also the wonderful Norwegians.

*

To revert, in the mid 1950s I was appointed Divisional Surveyor at Choma. Choma had a small, close-knit and friendly European population. There was no electricity, no piped water, no sewage system and no paved roads. There were no postal deliveries, indeed there were no postal deliveries anywhere in Northern Rhodesia. All mail - official and personal – was placed in a Post Office Box at the local post office, which was then regularly cleared by an African orderly. But on the whole life was sweet in Choma I made friends there who remained friends ever thereafter.

The young District Commissioner, F.M.B. (Mike) Russell was supportive and hospitable. He had an astonishing memory. When we staged an amateur production of a play, Mike was not only word perfect in his own part, after two readings of the play; he could also prompt all the other players who forgot their lines.

The Veterinary Officer was very short-sighted. He wore spectacles with thick lenses. The Africans called him *four eyes*! When we gave our young cat to him to have it castrated, *four eyes* shaved its abdomen in preparation for an operation on a female cat. His African assistant said "excuse me, Bwana, this is a tom cat"!

An African servant would go to the Choma village borehole with an empty 44 gallon drum, fill it with water, trundle it back to the house along the dirt roads, and pump the water from the drum into the water tank in the roof space. Lighting and refrigeration depended on paraffin. Sanitation necessitated the use of buckets housed in a small outhouse, which were emptied nightly. Cooking and heating (when necessary) were by wood, freely available from the surrounding bush and purchased by the "cord". I was fortunate in that I could often bring a load of firewood home on my truck, wood which had been felled in the course of my survey duties.

There was no church in Choma. There was an Anglican Mission Station some 20 miles away. James Robertson, the priest in charge of the mission, became a great friend. Every now and then, James would travel in to Choma to administer Holy Communion. Sometimes the service was held in our house, at other times in the house of another government officer. Dr. Temple, the Archbishop of Canterbury visited the Mission Station. James invited Jean and me to go to the Mission Station and receive the holy sacraments from the Archbishop, at 6 a.m. one day. Breakfast followed. James had then organised some tribal dancing to entertain the Archbishop and his wife. James's young daughter, Grace became very excited by the dancing. James said "Do, please sit down and be quiet, Grace". The Archbishop immediately responded "Is that how you speak to your Archbishop in Africa"?

A particular survey task I had to undertake in Choma was to define a boundary between Crown Land and the adjoining Native Reserve. The local Africans thought that there were encroachments into the Native Reserve. Fortunately, a local plan showed that there should be a survey beacon defining a boundary point between Crown Land and the Native Reserve. The local Africans were aware, of course, that there had been such a beacon. But where was it? I met a group of Africans at an agreed point, showed them my map and calculated that if they walked with me for a specified distance on a specified compass bearing, we ought to find that beacon. Off we all trudged. Fortunately, my calculations were accurate, the beacon was found, undisturbed. The Africans were most impressed: end of dispute!

When I left Choma, I got the following letter from my Senior African Assistant Surveyor. I was greatly touched. Dated 5 September 1955, it said:

> On behalf of the Survey staff and labourers I hereby give our sympathetic farewell to you.
>
> We first of all thank you very much for your good supervision you had on us throughout. You have taught us so many things which we did not know before. I must not forget the kindness you did to us in our individual troubles. These all have shown us the way in which white and black can work together.
>
> After all, you are now leaving us. We are very sorry for your going. It will take us time to expect the same treatment and kindness from

the coming new officer. May the Almighty God help you throughout your journey home, and have a good time, success and luck till you may come back again.
In conclusion, we all say Good-bye to you for ever and ever.

I am, Sir,

(Signed) James Hamainda

Next year, I had a letter from James's friend E.H. Chiswala, for whom I had secured a place at the African Survey Training School. He wrote: "It has been a very long time since I left you at Choma without writing to you a letter, but anyway, I still think of you very much and I may say it will take me a long time to forget you, Sir. I was and still am very pleased to be promoted to Scale B which I did not dream or expect much. So I say thank you for your earnest recommendation which I expect and trust you did it with all your heart. So, Sir, I don't know how I can express my thanks to your majesty, but God knows how much."

*

After Choma, my next appointment was Divisional Surveyor Lusaka. Lusaka was a bigger and busier office than Choma. I had three young European surveyors on my staff. One of these junior surveyors, a delightful young man of Rhodesian origin, went out shooting at night and bagged a female kudu. I was given a cut of venison. The owner of the farm where the animal was shot found out who the culprit was. Naturally, he raised merry hell, not only with me, but also with my head office. Eventually abject apologies and undertakings that the offence would not be repeated saved the day. I was relieved that no disciplinary action was taken against my young friend.

I blotted my copy-book more seriously, in a social sense. My next door neighbour was Major D.M. (Mike) Talmage. Mike was the local secretary of the Royal Commonwealth Society.

When he went on long leave, he asked me to hold the fort for him in Commonwealth Society affairs. I was a member of the Society: I readily agreed. I was told that there would be little to do. How wrong! One day the Governor's private secretary rang me up and told me that the Chairman of the Royal Commonwealth Society, Lord De La Warr was shortly visiting Lusaka with his wife. It was my responsibility to organise a reception for him. I said I was not prepared to do this, under any circumstance. The private secretary rang again. The Governor expected it of me. The reception would be funded by the government. I said I was sorry, but I was not prepared to do this. When I knew the date of De La Warr's visit, I wrote to him, explained the situation as tactfully as I could and invited him and his wife to have dinner with Jean and me at the Ridgeway Hotel. I had no reply. I then got an invitation to a reception at Government House, in order to meet De La Warr. Naturally, I had to accept. Shortly after my arrival at the reception, I approached De La Warr in order to offer my apologies. I suspect the Governor had asked his staff to keep a close eye on me. I had hardly introduced myself to De La Warr, when the Aide-de-Camp strode across the room, and whipped De La Warr away to meet another guest. Shortly afterwards, I resigned my membership of the Royal Commonwealth Society. There was silence from Government House.

It was not long before I was transferred from the Divisional Office in Lusaka to Departmental Headquarters, as Acting Chief Surveyor – third in the departmental hierarchy. By this time the Department of Surveys and Land had been split into the Survey Department (with Percy Allin as Surveyor General) and the Lands Department (with Bill Younger as Commissioner of Lands). Bill tried hard to persuade me to be his Deputy, even to the extent of speaking to Jean about it. As much as I liked and admired Bill, I felt I was at last making progress as a surveyor. Certainly, my relations with Percy Allin were far more cordial. S.G. (Sydney) Burlock, from the Provincial Administration, became the Deputy Commissioner of Lands.

Of course, my tenure of the post of Acting Chief Surveyor

came to an end when the substantive holder of that post, D.A. (Jock) Maclean returned from long leave. He was yet another South African land surveyor, a late arrival in Northern Rhodesia, but senior to me. Bill Younger got at me again and eventually persuaded me to take the post in the Lands Department of Principal Lands Officer and Executive Officer of the Agricultural Lands Board. In effect, I was the substantive third in seniority in the Lands Department.

At the same time, I kept a foot in the survey camp: I was elected the first President of the Land Surveyors' Society of Northern Rhodesia. There were several private practitioners engaged mostly in surveys for the government, under contract. The Society's main task seemed to be liaison between the private surveyors and the government, with a view to the government making amendments to the Land Survey Ordnance. (Amongst other matters, the Ordnance stipulated the fees that could be charged for property surveys).

*

It was fascinating work with the Agricultural Lands Board. Bill Younger was the Chairman of the Board, but most of the members were European farmers. The Board's main concerns were adjudicating on requests for government loans, allocating farms to new settlers and adjudicating on the transfer of government leasehold farms. European farming was increasingly becoming an important part of the national economy. The major crops were maize, tobacco and cattle.

There was an occasion when Bill Younger had to fly to Salisbury for a meeting with our Southern Rhodesian counterparts. Bill asked me to go with him, but I didn't play an active part in the discussions, as far as I can remember. Sir Edgar Whitehead, who was then the Prime Minister of Southern Rhodesia, was in the chair. A Southern Rhodesian civil servant said something which annoyed Sir Edgar. He (Sir Edgar) promptly took his hearing aid out of his ear and slapped it down on the table in front of him! The political member of our delegation was John Moffat who was our Minister of Agriculture and an elected member of the Legislative Council. Moffat was a descendent of the famous missionary Robert Moffat (1795-1883) whose daughter, Mary married David Livingstone (1813-1873).

There was a small group of European farmers farming in a Crown Land enclave at Fort Jameson (now Chipata) near the Nyasaland border. These farms were isolated and they were in the one area under pressure for further African settlement. It was considered that for both economic and security reasons the continued occupation of this land by European farmers was uncertain. It was proposed that the land should be made available for African settlement and that the European farmers should be bought out and, if so desired, resettled on other Crown Land nearer the line of rail. It was my duty to make all the necessary arrangements.

Some of the Fort Jameson farmers opted to resettle at Mkushi. This was a large block of Crown land lying some distance to the north-east of Lusaka. In 1949/1950 this block of land had been divided into farms ranging from 3,000 to 6,000 acres in extent, for cattle ranching. The scheme was not successful. In 1956, the Federal Government surveyed the soil fertility of the area and recommended that it should be re-planned into much smaller units (1,000 to 2,000 acres) which would be viable tobacco-growing farms. Would-be farmers were vetted by the Agricultural Lands Board. They had to possess £3,000 in capital (or £2,000 in cash and a full range of farming equipment) and have at least two years' experience of tobacco production. Each new farm was given road access, a water supply and 40 acres of cleared land.

After the resettlement of, or compensation paid to the Fort Jameson farmers had been brought to a successful conclusion, the Permanent Secretary of the Ministry of Land and Natural Resources, K.V. (Kenneth) Maguire wrote to Sydney Burlock (then the Acting Commissioner of Lands) "I should like to record my congratulations and thanks to Mr. Sutherland for the work he has put into the proposals for resettling Eastern Province farmers. To have convinced all the critics here and in Salisbury and then to have achieved a warm welcome in Fort Jameson is nothing short of a triumph".

I had a good relationship with Kenneth Maguire He was easy-going and a capable administrator. But I noted his propensity to take two days or so of sick leave when there was a particular knotty problem to be settled. The Assistant Secretary in the Ministry of Land and Natural Resources blotted his copy-book. Although a married man, he established a relationship with a male African security guard and was apprehended coupling with him one night. The reaction was swift. The Assistant Secretary resigned. He and his wife were provided with immediate passages back to Britain. I do not know the fate of the poor African concerned.

*

Bill Younger retired. Sydney Burlock stepped up as Commissioner of Lands and I stepped up as his Deputy. My duties then embraced the whole of the Department, including the Land Registry. We had a competent, hard-working staff. There were no difficulties that I can recall. When Sydney took his long leave, I acted as Commissioner of Lands for 6 months. I had to chair a committee which was investigating the surrender of more Crown Land, to African settlement. Members of the Provincial Administration who served on my Committee pressed hard for a reduction in the Crown Land estate. I was opposed. Agricultural development of Crown Land was becoming an important element in the territory's economy. I am sure the "Sutherland Report" was unpopular in the higher echelons of government, but I won the day. The Crown Land Estate was not pared (other than in the Fort Jameson area) and was in due course handed over to the independent Zambian government as state controlled land.

It is worth noting that all the water courses on Crown Land remained the property of the Crown. If a stream separated two farms, the boundaries of the farms on either side extended only as far as the bank of the stream, not to the thalweg. If an adjoining property owner wanted to extract water from the stream, he had to get a permit from the government Water Board.

Bill Younger was Chairman of this Board. Incidentally, the fact that the boundaries of the two farms were the two banks of the stream doubled the work of the land surveyor in depicting the farms' boundaries on the diagrams attached to their title deeds, and in assessing their acreages.

*

Another important duty which came my way was to find a site for a new, international airport at Lusaka. The existing airport was on the edge of the built-up area of Lusaka. It couldn't be expanded and it couldn't accommodate large planes I selected a new site on Crown Land a few miles east of the town. I invited the Director of Civil Aviation in Salisbury to come and have a look at it. He flew up to Lusaka in a small plane The two of us had a good look from the air at all the land surrounding Lusaka, The Director of Civil Aviation readily accepted the site I had suggested. That was that! There was no protracted planning inquiry. The land was immediately handed over to the Civil Aviation Department of the Federal Government and the new airport was built. Not for a moment did I imagine that it would be named after me, but it would have been a fine gesture had I been invited to the opening ceremony of *Lusaka International Airport*.

*

Many of the territorial boundaries of Northern Rhodesia were artificial and arbitrary. They had been imposed when the European colonising powers had divided up Africa between them. There were more than 50 different tribes within Northern Rhodesia, several with different languages, customs and cultures. Britain had held the country together, as one unit. Perhaps only a strong leader from the dominant tribe could continue to hold the country together, once it had become independent (Zambia). Kenneth Kaunda was such a leader. He soon became the leader of the non-official members of the Legislative Council and he was clearly destined to become Zambia's first President. In the event, he proved to be less despotic than some of the leaders emerging as Presidents elsewhere in independent African states.

Nevertheless, he made sure that his own tribe – the Bemba people – held suzerainty and he was ruthless with some of the other tribes who opposed him. It is a great mistake to think of the independent states in Africa as being democratic in the western tradition, that is with two or more parties opposing one another on *philosophical* principles. Throughout Africa, including South Africa, one man one vote simply results in the majority tribe dominating all others, based entirely on *tribal* customs and prejudices.

I met Kenneth Kaunda once or twice in the course of my duties, before Zambia got its independence in 1964. He listened to me politely. But it was clear that he didn't want any advice. His mind was already made up, as to what should be done.

Shortly before Zambia became an independent republic, there was a large meeting in Government House, chaired by the Governor (Sir Evelyn Hone), at which the future of Barotseland was to be discussed. Under colonial rule, Barotseland had special protectorate status. There was a resident District Commissioner and one or two other government officials, but essentially Barotseland was governed by its own parliament and king. The king was a British baronet – Sir Mwanawina Lewanika. He was descended from the Lewanika who had granted concessions to Cecil Rhodes. I was asked to attend this conference, presumably because African land rights were on the agenda. [In fact, I had no expertise in African land rights: my remit was solely for Crown Land administered under the British system of land tenure]. Naturally, Sir Mwanawina and Kenneth Kaunda were both at the conference. Sir Mwanawina was a dignified old man who commanded the loyalty and respect of a large tribe – the Barotse. Kenneth Kaunda was the up-and-coming self-assured politician. The central question was whether Barotseland should continue to enjoy its special protectorate status under an independent Zambia, or whether it should become an integral part of the new Zambia. It was quite obvious to me, as I listened to the debate that the Governor and his officials would agree to whatever Kenneth Kaunda wanted. **He** wanted Barotseland to be an integral part of

**his** new Zambia. And so it became. I am sure that poor old Sir Mwanawina had little idea of how much power and authority he would be losing. I was thoroughly disgusted that the British colonial officials had failed to support him.

*

The Federation of the two Rhodesias and Nyasaland broke up in 1963. Nyasaland was granted its independence. It was clear that Northern Rhodesia was also heading for independence. All this happened with great rapidity. Some Africans, who were not members of the dominant Bemba tribe, expressed to me their fears for the future. They pleaded that we (the colonial government) should stay.

But, egged on by the United States I believe, Harold Macmillan and Ian Macleod spear-headed a headlong dash towards the dismantlement of Britain's colonial empire and the granting of independence to all its colonial territories. When I had been interviewed for my first appointment in the Colonial Service, way back in 1948, I was asked to express my views on the future of the colonies. I could see that my answer didn't please the interviewing officer – a former colonial civil servant. I had replied that we had a duty to prepare our colonies for self-government **in the long term**. I hope therefore that I won't be accused of being a diehard when I say, categorically, that in the case of Northern Rhodesia independence in 1964 came far too soon. For a start, there was insufficient expertise amongst the indigenous population to run a municipality, let alone a country. Possibly not more than half a dozen Africans held university degrees. Secondly, African society was still overwhelmingly feudal in nature – paramount chiefs, lesser chiefs, elders, village headmen. Thirdly, as already pointed out, African society was divided on a predominantly tribal basis.

*

As independence loomed, I had to consider my own future. It was obvious that there would be little or no future for me in the new Zambian Civil Service. Already, I was training an African minister's cousin to take over my job as Deputy Commissioner of Lands. A number of colonial civil servants (by now called overseas civil servants) did stay on in Zambia for a few more years. I hope this eased the transition. But the majority of us left Zambia, under generous redundancy terms. I had just turned 38 when independence came. I felt that if I delayed repatriation until I was even older, my chances of getting a reasonable replacement post in England would become that much harder.

James Robertson, my friend from Choma days, was by now the Principal of the Technical College in Lusaka. The Technical College became the University of Zambia. James invited me to consider a teaching post at the University. I declined.

I expect our African Survey School, about which I have written previously, became a faculty of the new University. In the run-up to independence, one of the European staff at the School was instructing his African trainees in elementary trigonometry. He was having great difficulty in convincing one African that the tangent of an angle was the same as its sine divided by its cosine. According to the African, it was the other way round: the tangent was the cosine divided by the sine. Exasperated, the African finally said "when we get independence I shall be right and you will be wrong". Such was African naivety!

An "Independence Honours List" was drawn up. This had been the practice when other colonies became independent. But Kenneth Kaunda, clearly on the path to becoming Zambia's first President, would have none of it. No honour was awarded. I heard on the grapevine that my name had been put forward with a recommendation that I should be awarded the OBE. I probably didn't deserve it. I certainly never got it!

At a moving ceremony in October 1964, the Union Jack was lowered for the last time and the flag of Zambia was raised in its stead. The Zambian flag has three colours black, green and orange – black for the people, green for the bush, and orange for the rich copper deposits. "What about a little white for the whites" someone asked? The reply was "the flagpole is white and it is holding up all the rest"!

Outside the Secretariat buildings in Lusaka there was a replica of Watts's famous statue of a man on horseback, which is entitled *Physical Energy.* The original stands in Hyde Park Gardens, London: another replica stands at the Rhodes Memorial in Cape Town. The new Zambian government thought the statue was entitled *Physical **NRG**,* pretty close to Physical Energy! NRG was the abbreviation for Northern Rhodesia Government and was in frequent use. The statue was consequently promptly removed! It went to Salisbury (Harare).

I soldiered on in Zambia until the end of 1964. I applied for an appointment in the administrative branch of the home civil service. I had to take a written examination which seemed to be designed to test my command of English and my ability to analyse a written statement. I don't think I did too well. However, after I got back to England, the Home Civil Service put me through a 3 or 4 day test, similar to the WOSB tests that I had endured during my short army career. I will write more of that in the next chapter.

On Christmas Eve 1964, I attended midnight Holy Communion at Lusaka Cathedral. I left Zambia by train early on Christmas morning. A few people came to the station to bid me farewell. I have never returned to Zambia and never will. A country that once had a great future has squandered its potential, although it has fared rather better than many other former British colonies in Africa. However, when I look back I have to say that the years I spent in Northern Rhodesia were stimulating and most enjoyable.

I had come to have a great affection for the country and all its inhabitants. I was very fearful for its and their future. There is no satisfaction in saying that I firmly believe I was right to be fearful. It has been tragic to read of the degeneration in Zambia. It is painful to say that I have never wanted to return there. Perhaps I am at fault in once hoping that one day the country would become a great nation, with western ideals and principles. Perhaps Macmillan and Macleod were right in thinking (if they did) "let the African countries settle their own future however they will".

50. Voyage Home on First Leave 1952 – with Mother, Sister and Brother-in-law

51. Shadyhangar, Hascombe – Rented during First Leave

52. Author with Pam Richards, Livingstone 1952

53. J.A. (Paddy) and Dorothy White in old age ( 2000)

54. The Secretariat, Lusaka

55. Physical Energy (G.F. Watts) – Secretariat, Lusaka

56. Typical Anthill in Northern Rhodesia (built by termites)

57. Crown Land, Mkushi, Northern Rhodesia

58. Lusaka International Airport

59. President Kenneth Kaunda

## Chapter 9

# TRANSITION

I sailed for England and an uncertain future, on an Italian liner, from Durban. I was now sufficiently senior in the Overseas Civil Service to be able to travel first class.

During the voyage, news came through of the death of Sir Winston Churchill. His death was announced at lunch by a retired senior Air Force Officer, who called for a minute's silence. The captain of our ship was justifiably annoyed. It was *his* prerogative to make such an important announcement.

Some years later I was on a cruise when one of the guest speakers was John Cole – a retired BBC political correspondent. John had many amusing anecdotes. This is the anecdote he had about Churchill. Arrangements for the great man's state funeral had been drawn up some time before his death. A civil servant was detailed to clear these arrangements with Churchill. Churchill's only concern was that the train carrying his coffin from London to Bladon, in Oxfordshire, where he was to be buried, should start from Waterloo Station. "But, Sir" said the civil servant, timidly "I am afraid Oxfordshire trains don't use Waterloo Station". "Look here" said Churchill. "If De Gaulle comes to my funeral, we most definitely must start from Waterloo. If De Gaulle doesn't come to my funeral, the train journey may start wherever you damn well please"! In the event, De Gaulle did come to Churchill's funeral. The train journey started at Waterloo and the coffin was taken by special train and special route across London for the burial in Bladon.

I nipped in the bud a possible romance with an Italian princess, on this my last voyage from Africa to England as an Overseas Civil Servant. We dined together, we danced together, and we played bridge as partners. She told me my fortune with a pack of cards, which turned out to be fairly accurate. But I didn't allow my princess to become too intimate.

Reticence on my part was often a hindrance to my romances. I definitely preferred to be the hunter, not the quarry. The chase was sufficient attraction in itself. None of my romances ended in penetrative sex. I was far too inhibited.

There was a violent storm in the channel the night before we docked. The final celebrations on board were a shambles. Was this a bad omen as regards my future?

Aunt Moonie and her husband Harold gave me accommodation for a week or two. Jean had already returned to England and was staying with them. I then managed to rent, for 6 months, a charming furnished house with a most beautiful garden in Haselmere.

I was summoned, as I have mentioned previously, to a three-day interview board, to test my suitability for appointment as an administrative officer in the Home Civil Service. In one test, the candidates were divided into groups of 6 or 8 people and presented with a file of papers to study. We then had to make recommendations or judgments on the basis of what we had read. Each candidate, in turn, chaired a "meeting" comprised of the rest of the group. After discussion, the Chairman had to summarise what had been said, and come to his conclusion. I didn't find this difficult when I was Chairman. I had had plenty of experience of similar situations, in real life. A senior P.A. officer from Northern Rhodesia was in my group. He made a complete hash of chairing the meeting and had to be helped out by other members of the group, including me. I mention this, because eventually this P.A. officer was offered a (temporary) appointment in the Home Civil Service. I wasn't, as I shall make clear.

I passed all the tests and then had to appear before a Selection Board. The Board was chaired by a pleasant man who opened the proceedings by asking a few simple questions about my past experience. He then handed over the questioning to three of the other six members of the Board. In my case, the three questioners were a female academic (no problems there), a retired civil servant (considerable problems) and a trade union official (major problems).

It was clear that the retired civil servant (who was wearing his carpet slippers!) had been involved with the national housing programme. He wanted me to agree that this programme should have top priority in the government's expenditure plans. I disagreed. But was my disagreement sufficiently tactful? Probably not! The trade union official was downright rude. Having floored me with a technical question to which I should have known the answer, he accused me of being born with the proverbial silver spoon in my mouth, and having been an officer in the army and the Deputy Commissioner of Lands in Zambia simply as a result of patronage. It was not so. I bridled.

I came away from the Board thinking that I had almost certainly lost the support of two of the questioners. A week or two later I got a polite letter telling me that there was no vacancy for me in the administrative service at that time (coded rejection of my application), but offering me a job as a tax inspector. Not only was I disappointed, I was incensed. I returned the letter on which I wrote "if I had wanted a job as a tax inspector, I would have applied for one"! How regrettable! How rude!

The Overseas Service Resettlement Board then went to great lengths to find me an appointment. I was even sent on a short induction course to learn about private sector enterprise. At the same time, I scanned the *situations vacant* columns in the national press.

After one or two false starts, I was invited to an interview by the Chairman of the Housing Association. The Association was concerned with those people who could not afford to house themselves in the private housing market, but who didn't qualify for public sector housing. I got on well with the Chairman, a retired senior army officer. But the Secretary of the Association was altogether someone different – a career civil servant called Vipond, who clearly resented the possible intrusion of another "outsider". The Chairman gave me some draft housing legislation to read and comment on. This I did, probably incurring the further displeasure of Vipond.

Meanwhile I had applied on my own initiative for the post of Senior Administrative Officer in the Kent County Council Planning Department. An administrative job, working with professionals was, perhaps, something where my past experience would be telling. I was interviewed by the County Planning Officer (R.G. Clarke) and his Deputy (W.H. Deakin). It was clear that Deakin was the dominant personality. (Indeed, a year or two later Deakin, himself, became the County Planning Officer – a very able one).

Deakin quizzed me about my professional career. (I was now a Fellow of the RICS). He considered that I would be more suited to a professional, than to an administrative post in the Planning Department. He said that the Department already had a qualified surveyor on its professional staff, who would become a planning officer as soon as he had obtained his membership of the Royal Town Planning Institute (RTPI). He said that my professional qualification (FRICS) would probably give me exemption from part of the RTPI syllabus. Once I had a planning qualification to supplement my survey qualification, my prospects in the Planning Department would be good. The administrative appointment in the Planning Department, on the other hand, was a dead end job. Would I think this over? If I was interested in an appointment as a Survey Assistant in the Department, I should let the County Planning Officer know. Perhaps, it was suggested, I should like to discuss all this with Rex Mercer, the surveyor currently on the Departmental planning staff. Rightly or wrongly (wrongly, as it turned out), I gained the impression that if I obtained my RTPI qualification, my past career and experience would be taken into account, and a suitable post would be offered to me when one became available.

I discussed this with Rex Mercer, who was well on his way to obtaining a Diploma in Town Planning at University College, London. Rex suggested that I should follow suit. Rex was clearly very capable and he was a likeable chap. Later we became good friends.

I wrote to the County Planning Officer to say that I

should be pleased to be appointed as a Survey Assistant in his Department. Immediately after this acceptance, I received an offer for the vacant post with the Housing Association. Regretfully, I had to decline. One factor that weighed heavily with me was that it would be much more pleasant working in Kent, than commuting to the Housing Association's head office, which was located far from the centre of London.

Kent became my home for the next 35 years.

60. April Cottage, Haslemere – Rented in 1965

Chapter 10

# KENT

When I started working for the Kent Planning Department, my lease of April Cottage, Haselmere, still had a few weeks to run. The new house I was purchasing in Maidstone was not yet ready for occupation. As a result, I became a weekly commuter. I lived in the Star Hotel in Maidstone (since closed) from Monday to Friday and returned to Haselmere at the weekend. My new house was still unfinished when my Haselmere lease expired, so Jean and I lived as permanent but temporary residents in the Star Hotel for a few weeks. Then we moved into 20 Saxons Drive, the end building in a three-storey terrace. It was built of brick with white weather-boarding - traditional Kentish building materials - and it had quite a lot of glass, all under a tiled roof. There was a built-in garage, a utility room and a cloak room on the ground floor; a living room, kitchen and larder on the first floor, and three small bedrooms and a bathroom on the top floor. The living room faced south. Its glass windows covered virtually the whole frontage of the house, from wall to wall and from ceiling to floor. The kitchen faced north and afforded a splendid view of the North Downs – until my neighbour to the north sold his tennis court and some garden to a developer who promptly built two new houses. No more view! My house had a small garden on three sides. Saxons Drive was a small cul-de-sac. Number 20 was at the head of the cul-de-sac. Therefore there was no noise from traffic. My terrace was sited in the north-west corner of a former (Victorian?) estate called *Foley Park*. Lengths of the old 6-foot brick wall which had enclosed Foley Park became my boundaries to the west and to the north. My south frontage was open-plan, facing the cul-de-sac. On the other side of the western boundary wall was a footpath. Along the path to the north it was a 5 minute walk to Penenden Heath, with its small shopping centre, pub and large open space frequented by soccer players, cricketers and children in their play area. Centuries back, Penenden Heath had been a site for the County Assize Court. Offenders who were sentenced to death were hanged on the crest of the hill not far from Saxons Drive. It is still called *Gallows Hill.*

To the south, the footpath outside my western boundary led to another small shopping area, which we patronised. From there it was a 12 minute walk to my office in County Hall, with Maidstone East railway station just further on. It was an ideal location for me. 20 Saxons Drive was Jean's home until the year before her death in 1979. It was my home for 35 years. I had commuted into a lump sum the maximum permitted proportion of my Zambian pension. This sum enabled me to make a deposit on the purchase of 20 Saxons Drive and to furnish it. All the furniture, hard and soft, came from *Maple*, in London – an excellent firm with whom to deal.

*

Following the example of Rex Mercer, I applied for a place on the next available Town Planning diploma course at University College, London. I had quite a tussle, but eventually secured a place. Rex, of course was two years in advance of me, but we often travelled together from Maidstone to London for our evening lectures.

In the Planning Department, Rex and I worked in what was called the *Urban Planning Group.* Our principal task at that time was the re-planning of major town centres. There were two main reasons why this re-planning was necessary: first, to make provision for the burgeoning amount of road traffic; secondly to accommodate major new shopping developments. Rex was working on the re-planning of Ashford town centre. In my view, he outshone, both in ability and in industry, the other members of the Urban Planning Group, notwithstanding that most of them were already fully qualified chartered town planners, and Rex wasn't.

Rex apart, I was staggered by the lack of industry in the Urban Planning Group. People arrived late, took long lunch and coffee breaks and thought nothing of a shopping expedition during working hours. I was used to a hard day's work. There was virtually nothing for me to do in the Urban Planning Group. I was given Colin Buchanan's *Traffic in Towns* to read and that was that. I found the lack of work most frustrating.

*

After a while, I was given the task of assessing the amount of new shopping development which could reasonably be permitted, first in Tunbridge Wells and later in Deal. The local councils of both towns were very keen to permit major new shopping centres. I had little faith in my complicated calculations which suggested, in both towns, that new shopping centres of the magnitude sought could not be justified by the estimated future demands. I was more concerned, however, that the proposed development in Tunbridge Wells would have an adverse impact on the future of *The Pantiles* and of the High Street, and that the proposed development in Deal was out of character with the small-scale character of this charming seaside town. In neither case were my objections supported by Tony Walton (my boss), whose natural instinct was not to cross swords with the officers of another local authority.

*

I was pleased to be transferred to the Maidstone Development Control office. Here there was an abundance of work. *Development Control* consisted essentially of examining applications for planning permission, consulting other authorities and interested parties on the merits or demerits of each application, and then reporting the application to a committee of elected members with a recommendation for approval, approval with conditions, or refusal. The decision of the committee would be notified to the applicant by the Clerk of the County Council. It was essential to keep a record of all planning applications and decisions relating to every land parcel. The major boroughs in Kent were autonomous for most development control in their bailiwicks; the County Council was fully responsible for all development control in rural district council areas.

I have to say that there was also a degree of frustration

working on development control, although it was nowhere near as bad as the amount of frustration I had felt, through under-utilisation, in the Urban Planning Group. Development Control, in essence, was a clerical job, with little scope for professional judgment. There were 101 consultees whose views had to be taken into account (and reported to the committee) before making a recommendation. Some of these consultees were other members of the Department (e.g. the Chief Architect). The list of internal consultees was so long that I once had my knuckles rapped for writing at the end of the list *Uncle Tom Cobley and All*! It seemed that I had no personal discretion.

There was no fee, in the 1960s, for lodging an appeal to central government against the County Council's refusal to grant planning permission. Appeals were numerous. One was often asked to represent the County Council in an appeal against a decision in which one had played no part. I enjoyed appeal work. For once, no other officer or member of the Council was breathing down my neck. I stood alone. If I thought that the permission should have been granted in the first place, I could refuse to take the appeal. This happened only once. On another occasion, I declined to take an appeal because the government planning inspector had been a colleague of mine in the army. I am proud to say that I never lost an appeal.

I once had the temerity to challenge the opinion of the Department's Chief Architect, George Smith. (His nickname was *Noobs*, because he frequently wrote "No Obs"- i.e. no observations, when he was consulted). Many houses in the Weald of Kent were of medieval origin, with later alterations. An application to alter a medieval house near Cranbrook included the replacement of its sash windows on the Georgian façade with diamond leaded windows of pseudo-Tudor appearance. George told the applicants that he had no objection. I told George that I intended to call on the applicants in an endeavour to persuade them to leave the windows as they were. Their proposal, in my view, was not in keeping with the Georgian front. The applicants said that it was a medieval cottage and that diamond leaded windows would be in keeping. George said, quite correctly, that the panes in the existing sash windows were not to the standard Georgian dimensions. The applicants wouldn't recant. The sash windows were removed: diamond leaded windows were inserted. Every time thereafter, when I drove past this house, I averted my gaze!

*

One interesting duty allotted to me when I was working on development control, was to advise on all matters relating to trees: should trees on a site where development was proposed be retained; were they so important that they should be the subject of a *Tree Preservation Order*; should the planting of new trees be a condition of planning consent? A further interesting task in relation to trees was to advise on the landscaping of a section of a new motorway in Kent (part of the M20).

One day I noted that a few yew trees had been felled not far from Maidstone, in the North Downs Area of Outstanding Natural Beauty (AONB). The Downs had long lost most of their tree cover: the few remaining trees were significant features in the landscape. I spoke to the farmer (Hughie Batchelor) who had recently acquired the land. He argued that yew trees were a weed and were a danger to his cattle. I told him that his new farm lay in an AONB. He should consult the County Council before felling any more trees on his land. Some months later, I had a telephone call from Tony Walton (by that time Deputy County Planning Officer) telling me that an irate County Councillor had spotted the felling of some beech trees on Batchelor's farm. Would I please take any necessary action? I left a message for Batchelor saying that felling should stop immediately and that the remaining beech trees in the grove were to be the subject of a Tree Preservation Order (TPO). I convened a site meeting which was attended by Batchelor, his contractor and by County and District Council members and officers. It was agreed that the remaining beech trees should be the subject of a TPO. I also extracted from Batchelor an undertaking to plant some new trees in the AONB, alongside the A249 Maidstone/Sittingbourne Road.

That was not the end of the matter. The County Council decided to prosecute Batchelor. In fact, because of the niceties of the law, it was Batchelor's contractor who was prosecuted. He was fined £50. No doubt Batchelor paid the fine, but still had a profit from the sale of the felled timber.

There was a sequel! I was walking one evening with a friend along a footpath crossing Batchelor's land, when we decided to shorten our walk and cut across a field to rejoin the Pilgrims' Way Who should appear while we were trespassing than Bachelor, driving a land rover? Now he will get his revenge, I thought. Not a bit of it. He was courtesy itself. He made no complaint and directed us to the nearest exit onto the Pilgrims' Way.

*

After I had returned from the Maidstone Development Control Office to the Urban Planning Group, I was given the task, together with Valerie Carter, of planning a major new residential area in Maidstone on undeveloped land, formally Vinter's Park. That was a job I thoroughly enjoyed. Another interesting assignment which came my way was to liaise with the architect Frederick McManus and the artist Gordon Cullen who were commissioned by the County Council to undertake a townscape appraisal of Tenterden. Their report *Tenterden Explored* was published to great acclaim. Through McManus, I met Sir Nicholas Pevsner socially. His series *The Buildings of England* is a classic.

There was a large area of land at Walderlade, on the outskirts of Chatham, which had been divided, after World War I, into lots of upwards of an acre, and sold off cheaply, often to Londoners visiting the area on day trips. Most of these plots were undeveloped. The ownership of many of them could not be traced. A few plots had shacks on them, some of which were occupied, whether legally or not. The County Council decided to acquire the whole area, by compulsory purchase, and re-plan it to modern residential standards. I was instrumental in the re-planning.

There was a major public inquiry into the County

Council's proposals. The Council engaged the services of a leading barrister, skilled in planning law and practice, to present its case. The case opened with a statement by the County Planning Officer (R.G. Clarke). The statement had been drafted for him and had been cleared by the barrister. Clarke was then questioned by a barrister representing some of the objectors. He made such a poor showing that the County's barrister said forthrightly that in no circumstances should he (Clarke) appear on the witness stand again! During the course of the inquiry, I had to give evidence. Our barrister tried to get me to agree that part of the new development would be seen by traffic on the M2 motorway, unless a belt of trees was retained. I was very familiar with the area, by now, and was confident that our barrister was mistaken. I wouldn't allow him to persuade me to his point of view. I am glad to say that, unlike Clarke, I was not barred from giving further evidence! In the end, the County Council's Compulsory Purchase Order was confirmed. Walderslade became a flourishing residential district. Some years later (1985) the Chief Executive of the County Council wrote "I well remember the [inquiry] and your very successful evidence".

*

After three years' study at University College, London, I obtained my Diploma in Town Planning. My thesis was on Urban Conservation. The conservation of areas of architectural and historic interest was becoming an increasingly popular policy. When my thesis was scrutinised, one of the examiners said, rather scathingly, "it is clear to me that you are a surveyor" - by implication, not a planner! The other examiner was more supportive. He suggested that, with a few alterations, the thesis should be published as a book. It never was. The next step was my election as a member of the Royal Town Planning Institute. Some years later, I was advanced to Fellow.

I was now aged 44 and a fully qualified town planner. I hoped that my progress in the Planning Department would be rapid and would take into account my years of service in the Overseas Civil Service in a kindred profession. It was not to be. I was deeply offended when my only rewards were to become a Planning Officer (instead of a Survey Assistant) on the Department's establishment and to have the date of my next annual increment advanced by 6 months. Thus, I would have to compete for promotion within the Department with other newly qualified town planners of not much more than half my age. I said nothing, but found it hard to forgive Harry Deakin for such miserable treatment. Bitterly, I reflected on my initial interview with him in 1965 when a bright future was intimated, once I qualified.

The Department underwent a major expansion, sometime later. It was quite unjustified, in my view, in terms of the Department's responsibilities and workload. It was empire building, pure and simple. I and several other Planning Officers were promoted to become Divisional Planning Officers. I stayed at that level for the remainder of my career in Kent. I had been, it will be recalled, the Deputy Head of a Government Department in Northern Rhodesia (Zambia). Between my lowly status as a Divisional Planning Officer in Kent and the rank of Deputy County Planning Officer were the ranks of Assistant County Planning Officer (of which there were several) and Principal Assistant County Planning Officer.

Local Government was reorganised in 1974. Many planning powers which had been exercised by the County Council were transferred to newly created District Councils. The County Planning Department was reorganised. We all had to re-apply for our posts. Here was my opportunity, I thought. I applied for the post of Principal Assistant County Planning Officer, and failing that, as Assistant County Planning Officer, Strategic Planning. It was a futile attempt. It was abundantly clear that the way in which all the senior appointments were to be filled, down to Assistant County Planning Officer, had been decided in advance. All that was necessary was for a couple of councillors to endorse these in-house decisions, which they did. To add to my wounds, D.J. (Dave) Nessling was appointed to the post of Assistant County Planning Officer, Strategic Planning.

Although a most pleasant man and in many ways a most able planner, Dave freely acknowledged that he would be at sea with his new portfolio of strategic planning. Indeed, he shortly left the service of the County Planning Department and became the Borough Planning Officer at Gravesend (Gravesham District Council). His post in the Department as Assistant County Planning Officer was abolished. I had to take over his strategic planning responsibilities, with no promotion to Assistant County Planning Officer..

Before that, I had to soldier on as a Divisional Planning Officer under C.D. (David) Sayers, the Assistant County Planning Officer responsible for environmental planning. David was a pleasant, hard-working and competent man, a good deal younger than me. He realised how frustrated I was, and gave me a pretty free rein. As well as several Planning Officers under my direction, I had a number of qualified Architects – but not *Noobs*! George Smith had become Maidstone Borough Council's Director of Planning.

I, too, had applied for the Maidstone post which George Smith got. The Chairman of the Maidstone Borough interviewing committee made it quite plain that he wanted an architect to fill the post. I refrained from pointing out that I already had several architects working under my direction, and that the head of a department had major responsibilities beyond the professional skills of an architect. The Chairman of the Borough Council's interviewing committee was also a County Councillor. He was called Nightingale. I will speak of him later.

I also applied in 1974/75 for Chief Planning Officer posts at Ashford, at Tunbridge Wells and at Loddon (Norfolk) – all without success.

*

I was pleased that one of my responsibilities while I was working under David Sayers was the designation of areas of special architectural or historic interest, known as *Conservation Areas*. Most of the groundwork of inspection and assessment was undertaken by my small team of architects. They knew the exacting standards I required. Nevertheless, I made it my duty to visit each and every proposed Conservation Area, before a recommendation was made to Council members. Only very occasionally, did I have to suggest minor alterations to the boundaries proposed by an architect.

In 1972, I had written a report on Conservation Areas. When I was recuperating after an operation, I received the following note from the County Planning Officer: "you will be pleased to know that the report you drafted on Conservation Areas was very well received by the Planning Committee. Members are very interested in these matters".

All the **towns** in Kent had one or more Conservation Areas, approved and designated. Kent also abounds in historic **village** settlements, with beautiful churches and old houses. So the core areas of many villages were also designated as Conservation Areas A village on the North Downs where County Councillor Nightingale lived (in a Grade II listed building) was surveyed, but rejected as a potential Conservation Area. I was summonsed to see the Deputy County Planning Officer (who was now Tony Walton). "Don't you realize", Walton said "that County Councillor Nightingale lives in this village? He is a keen conservationist". I replied "my recommendations are not based on who lives in a village, but solely on the architectural and historic qualities of the place. In my view, the village where County Councillor Nightingale lives does not have the necessary qualities. I am sorry, but I cannot recommend its designation as a Conservation Area". There the matter remained, until … some years later, District Councils were given the power to designate Conservation Areas. They were far less rigorous in their views than I had been. My guess is that Nightingale's village was designated as a Conservation Area, by *Maidstone Borough Council*! It will be recalled that Nightingale was a Borough Councillor as well as a County Councillor.

*

I greatly admired J.M. (Martin) Simmons who deservedly got the job of Principal Assistant County Planning Officer in 1974, when I also applied for it. Martin combined great intelligence with considerable industry. He was junior to me in age and in managerial experience, but senior to me in our profession as Town Planners. After securing the post, Martin ably led the group of County and District Planning Officers who prepared the County Structure Plan. He had in R.C. (Bob) Carter a Divisional Planning Officer who was a competent statistician, and who was an expert on all aspects of population growth or decline and on historic and possible future trends in Kent's economy. As I have mentioned previously, Martin roped me in as his Divisional Planning Officer, Strategic Planning, after Dave Nessling (who had held the post as an Assistant County Planning Officer – a grade senior to mine) had left. I greatly enjoyed working for Martin. I was ably supported by a team of brilliant young Planning Officers, of whom at least two went on to achieve great success in careers outside Kent.

I had only one minor altercation with Martin. We both signed our memoranda *MS.* Perhaps I had initialled something with an *MS* which was attributed to Martin, to his consternation. Martin wrote me a note asking me to change the way I initialled my work. I replied: "Martin! I am **M. S**utherland. You, in fact, are **J. S**immons. Furthermore, I have been M.S. longer than you have been (J).M.S. I shall continue to initial my work MS". Nothing more was said!

*

Earlier in his planning career, Martin Simmons had been seconded by Kent County Council to a regional planning organisation responsible for the strategic planning of the whole of the South East of England, extending from Bedfordshire to Hampshire and including Greater London (and Kent). After this organisation had produced the *Strategic Plan for the South East,* Martin returned to Kent. The Strategic Plan, like all plans needed to be reviewed and possibly modified in the light of unforeseen changing circumstances. There was a small core secretariat with offices in Queen Anne Street in central London, but it's number needed to be supplemented, from time to time, from secondments from the

Greater London or constituent County planning departments. I have no doubt that it was because Martin had been such a success when he worked for *SCLSERP* (as the organisation was then called), that Con Saunders, the charming director of SCLSERP, asked Kent for another secondment. The lot fell to me.

I have to say that, when I arrived in London (commuting daily from Maidstone), SCLSERP didn't seem to know what my task(s) should be. It was just like my early days in Kent Planning Department! Soon, however, I was hard at it. My main task was to assess the impact on the S.E. Region of the completed or emerging county structure plans, including the Greater London plan. This work was an essential input to the preparation of the revision of the S.E. Regional Plan. SCLSERP (later renamed *SERPLAN)* was an extremely bureaucratic organisation. There were mountains of reports to be written and digested, many committees to be served and frequent committee meetings. Any revised Regional Plan had to be broadly acceptable to all the local authorities in the South East, if it was to mean anything at all.

I came to the conclusion that Martin Simmons had adopted and modified many of SCLSERP's organisational techniques when he was given the job of preparing Kent's new County Structure Plan. I, for my part, set up a comprehensive monitoring system at SERPLAN, so that the Regional Plan could be kept under constant (instead of periodic) review. Kent planning department and other planning departments in the South East followed suit, when it came to keeping their own structure plans under review.

It was a great experience working for SCLSERP/ SERPLAN, not least because the core officers and staff were such delightful colleagues. It was rewarding to have such close relations with all the planning authorities in the South East, and to meet so many "outside" consultees, not least the civil servants in the Department of the Environment.

London's future and London's problems had a direct impact on the rest of the South East: hence the need for a regional strategy. The Greater London Council's (GLC's) powers as a planning authority had to take account of and mesh with the planning of the other authorities in the South East. Nevertheless, the GLC was the major planning authority. It acted as SCLSERP/ SERPLAN's quartermaster and paymaster.

Ken Livingstone, at this time, was the Chairman of the GLC. As far as I was able to judge, he was both efficient and effective. But he was a labour politician, whereas the government of the day was conservative, under the premiership of Margaret Thatcher. Figuratively speaking, poisoned arrows seemed to fly across the Thames between the House of Commons on the north bank and County Hall on the south bank. It was no surprise when Margaret Thatcher decided that the GLC was an unnecessary tier of local government and that it should be abolished. What would be the consequences for SERPLAN? Essex took over the role of quartermaster and paymaster, but staff and other retrenchments seemed inevitable. I was not on SERPLAN's permanent staff. I was only seconded, from Kent. I was advised to return to Kent. This I did. The Secretary of SERPLAN wrote "what I and your colleagues have valued in the professional aspect of our relationship has been your enthusiasm, your dedication to the concept of regional planning, and your passionate concern to maintain the highest standards of performance. We have admired your tenacity in discussion, your ability to perceive the need for action and to take that action swiftly and effectively, and your impressive range of technical and professional skills".

*

Unfortunately for me, the Kent Planning Department didn't have a suitable vacancy for me to fill. Clearly, it would have been inequitable to the sitting incumbent if I had returned to my position as Divisional Planning Officer, Strategic Planning. A job in the Countryside Division, under Chris Waite, was suggested. I declined, because it would prejudice the career prospects of another deserving Planning Officer. I returned to my original post of Divisional Planning Officer in David Sayer's Environmental Planning Division. But the tasks that I had previously performed in that Division had all but disappeared. Two makeshift tasks were found.

It was clear that members of the County Council were looking for savings. One idea that was being floated was to merge the Highways and Planning Departments. The two departments already shared an office block. In theory, a merger should result in saving the salaries of one head and one deputy head of a department, and a reduction in the number of administrative and clerical staff. It was also a well established fact that land use and highway planning were closely inter-related. Highway engineering, on the other hand stood on its own The Highways Department was dominated by qualified engineers.

Graham Good, an engineer in the Highways Department, and I were detailed to report on the feasibility of merging the two departments. Graham was a delightful, intelligent and easy person with whom to work. We took evidence from numerous officers in both departments, and in the County Clerk's Department. The consensus view, as was to be expected, was that the two departments should not be merged at that time.

Graham and I became known as *Gilbert and Sullivan*! Consequently we quoted freely from the libretti of the Gilbert and Sullivan operettas in the chapter headings to our report.

We reflected the consensus view in our recommendations. I am certain this cut no weight with the local politicians. But I hope our report was a learning exercise for those members who had the patience to read it. Inevitably, our report was shelved and private consultants were engaged.

The other interesting, though minor task given to me was to organise the annual three-day tour of the county, by the Chairman of the Town Planning Committee accompanied by the County Planning Officer.

*

An Assistant County Planning Officer post became available in the Countryside Division of the Department, when an old-timer retired. Clearly, the front runner to fill this vacancy was C.R. (Chris) Waite, the Divisional Planning Officer in that Division.

However, nothing daunted, I decided that I would also apply for the vacant post. Shortly before we were to be interviewed, I overheard the Departmental Secretary advising Chris Waite on the telephone to stand by for a meeting of all the Assistant County Planning Officers which was scheduled to take place a day or two after the interviews. It was obvious that it was not a two-horse race, with one favourite: the favourite had already passed the winning post. I withdrew my application. Tony Walton, the Deputy County Planning Officer, asked me why. I said simply "I don't think I have a chance". I was pressed to explain why I thought this. So I told Tony about the telephone call. I told him, furthermore, that I believed that Chris had been advised to hang on when the Assistant County Planning Officer posts were filled in 1974, because the officer who got the post in the Countryside Division was due to retire shortly. It was clear that Chris considered he had good prospects in Kent. He had not, like many of us, applied for posts outside the County Council: he had built an extension to his house in Maidstone. Both Tony Walton and the County Planning Officer assured me that it was an open competition. Frankly, I did not believe them and I told them so. I am pleased to record that Chris Waite was appointed and made an excellent Assistant County Planning Officer. He was awarded the OBE before he retired.

What then? I was aged 59. There was no prospect of promotion in the remaining years before my retirement. The Department was clearly searching around to find gainful employment for me. So when it was suggested that I might like to take a redundancy package, I accepted. Negotiations over the redundancy package were fraught. Kent said my County pension had to be reduced because I was already in receipt of a Zambian pension. I pointed out that there was a complete break between my Zambian and my Kent appointments. What I had done before joining Kent's pay role was no concern of Kent's and had not weighed, in any way, in my career with Kent. Kent had given me no credit for my Zambian service, neither when I was appointed, nor subsequently. The matter was referred to the

Home Office, goodness knows why! Eventually a compromise was reached. I retired. The Chairman of the Development Planning and Transportation Committee wrote “twenty years is a very long time to give to one organisation and I know that this has been both distinguished and characterised by a very special style and quality which you have brought to your work”. Harry Deakin wrote “may I say a strong personal thank you for the very considerable contribution you have made to the work and achievements of the Planning Department over the twenty years you have been here. Your time with Kent has been particularly marked by the wholehearted way you have given of your energy and abilities and I am most grateful for the positive and progressive approach that you have followed in all your work here”.

*

Shortly after I had retired, W.M. (Bill) Hopkins, the County Secretary invited me to help his department in dealing with the considerable extra workload which had occurred, as a result of the proposal to construct a Channel Tunnel. I gladly accepted, provided my pension arrangements with the County Council would not be affected. I wished to be paid as if I was on contract, not as a re-engaged member of staff. This was agreed, but the County Treasurer stipulated it could only be half-time employment.

I greatly enjoyed working in Bill Hopkins’ office. But I soon found that I was working full time, indeed more than full time. I suggested that the County Secretary should engage a full time assistant on the permanent staff. I felt that I was standing in the way. Bill Hopkins accepted my point. I left the employ of the County Council for the second – but not the last time.

There was an unusual incident. The woman in charge of the typists and clerical officers took a great fancy to me. I was quite unaware of this until one day when we were alone in the photo-copying room; she flung her arms around me, gave me a big hug and told me how wonderful I was! I didn’t respond in the way she obviously wished, but I hope I treated her kindly.

*

SERPLAN then offered me a contract to prepare a Waste Disposal Plan for the South East Region. I happily accepted. It was great to be back with my SERPLAN colleagues of former days. It was an interesting assignment. As can be imagined, the amount of waste generated in Greater London creates massive disposal problems. Land-fill sites in the rest of the region had to be used. They were being filled at an alarming rate. With the concurrence of all the local authorities in the South East Region, I was able to make several recommendations, but I felt that more radical solutions were needed.

*

No sooner had I completed my SERPLAN contract, than Bill Hopkins rang me again. The Channel Tunnel Bill was shortly to be considered by a Select Committee of the House of Commons. The County Secretary wanted someone to attend all the Committee hearings and to co-ordinate the County Council's manifold interests in the Bill. Not only were there major planning and highway concerns, but there were also questions of policing and fire safety. Hopkins wanted me to take on this job. "Would it be a full time job"? "Yes". "Would it attract a reasonable fee"? "Yes". "Would the County Treasurer lay down restrictions"? "No". So, of course, I accepted what turned out to be a very generous offer.

Some seven or eight Members of Parliament sat on the Select Committee. They conducted themselves as if they were a court of law. The main witnesses – the Government, the construction company, Kent County Council, and so on – had to address the Committee through a barrister. However, the Committee did deign to let individual objectors to the project address them directly, or through their solicitors, surveyors or the like. The County Council had to engage a top ranking barrister with experience of planning law and practice. The barrister would not accept a brief from the County's own solicitors: the County had to engage a London firm of solicitors who dealt with parliamentary procedures. In essence, it was a field day for the legal profession!

Although it was a Government Bill, the Government itself had to address the Select Committee through a barrister who was not in Government employ. He was Michael Fitzgerald. I shall write more on him, later.

It was fascinating work for me. I was given a House of Commons pass and was able to take meals in the Members' dining room. If we needed to have extra discussions with our barrister or solicitor or a senior County officer, I arranged for us to meet over lunch in the dining room of the Chartered Surveyors Institution, conveniently located on the other side of Parliament Square. I commuted daily to London when the Select Committee was sitting. I travelled first class. Once when I needed to discuss matters with our lawyers in their chambers, late in the evening, I stayed the night in London in a first class hotel, at the County's expense. This was the life! I was sorry when it was all over. Bill Hopkins wrote "I should like to thank you very much indeed for all the work you have done in your recall to duty. I do not know what we would have done without you".

*

That was the end of my career in public service. With only two small breaks between appointments, it had lasted from 1944 until 1986 – 42 years. I continued to live in Kent until the year 2000. Then I moved to Aldeburgh, on the Suffolk coast. In the remaining chapters of this book, I shall say a few words about Aldeburgh and then describe some of my recreational activities. But first, a small incident relating to my old school, Dover College.

*

I was having an interval drink, one evening, at the Marlowe Theatre in Canterbury, when a man approached me and said "is that an Old Dovorian tie you are wearing"? I looked down and said "yes". He introduced himself. He was Patrick Dudgeon, at that time the housemaster of School House at Dover College. Patrick is a most hospitable man – and a good cook. He invited me to come to the College and have dinner with him. I arrived at dusk. What a change from my days at the College. The school was now co-educational. Boys and girls were in various embraces in the college close. Patrick's dinner guests included the Head Girl. The rest of us were at least a generation older than she was. I felt rather sorry for her. Perhaps Patrick did, too. When we made our farewells, Patrick gave her a big kiss! Not to be outdone, I immediately kissed the Rector's wife, which raised an eyebrow or two, I suspect!

*

Jean, my mother, was in declining health at the end of the 1970s and had to be moved into a local Nursing Home. Her GP rang me at the beginning of 1979 to tell me that she had pneumonia. He could prescribe for her condition, but in six months time there would undoubtedly be another episode of pneumonia. She had no enjoyment in her life in the nursing home, the GP said. Should he let her slip away peacefully? I agreed. She died on 22nd February 1979. Although her departure from this life gave me the freedom which I had lost in 1951 – she lived with me and depended entirely on me in the intervening years- I naturally felt her loss deeply. I had her ashes scattered on the grave of her parents in Pett Church graveyard, near Hastings.

Chapter 11

# ALDEBURGH

*The Sea! The Sea!*

Northern Rhodesia is a land-locked country. The only sea that I saw during my 16 years' service in Northern Rhodesia was during my spells of overseas leave. During my earlier service in the Royal Engineers, I had seen the Mediterranean, I had swum in the Dead Sea and I had sailed and swum in the Great Bitter Lake in Egypt. In my youth, I had lived for a few years, in sight of the sea, near the East Sussex coast. My boarding school was in the seaside port of Dover, but while I was a boarder the school moved to an inland location in Devon. When I worked in Kent I lived in Maidstone, far from the sea. In a later chapter, it will become clear that my love of the sea was assuaged by many cruises. But since 2000 I have been fortunate to have lived right beside the North Sea in the charming small town of Aldeburgh.

For several years when I was still living in Maidstone, I visited Aldeburgh annually in order to attend concerts in the June International Music Festival (see chapter 12). When an Aldeburgh Prom season was started in August each year, in the concert hall at Snape (just outside Aldeburgh), my Aldeburgh visits became twice yearly. I got to know Aldeburgh and the surrounding countryside well.

In 1999, I learnt that *English Courtyard* was to build a new development of semi-sheltered housing in Aldeburgh. I had met Shuttleworth, the founder and chairman of *English Courtyard* and I had seen their housing developments at Lenham in Kent and elsewhere. I was impressed. *English Courtyard* houses and flats are costly to buy (on 99-year leases), but with the generous help of Heather I was able to afford the purchase of a 2-bedroom house in *English Courtyard's* Aldeburgh development.

In an *English Courtyard* development one has complete independence inside one's own property (which may include a small patio garden), but there is an on-site management team who is responsible for the upkeep of the exterior of all buildings and the maintenance of the communal garden. One of the managers also has to be available to respond to any emergency call from a resident. Residents, of course, have to pay an annual fee for these services.

Alas, it has to be said that the Aldeburgh development failed to reach the high standards achieved elsewhere by *English Courtyard*. The designs of the buildings and of the general layout of the grounds were as good as ever, but the actual building construction left a lot to be desired. The root cause was probably due to the fact that a reputable firm of builders was not employed. Instead *English Courtyard* relied on part-time building labourers under the overall supervision of a clerk of works. Shortly after I took up residence in June 2000, only about a third of the development had been completed. The clerk of works was fired because he was a drug addict. His replacement lived in Dorset. He would arrive on site late on a Monday afternoon and leave for home early on Friday. Effectively, therefore, he worked for only three days a week. In no way could he give proper attention to the work in progress. Indeed, I never once saw him going round and inspecting the work. Moreover I never saw, on site, the architects who had designed the development. Added to this lack of supervision, there is little doubt that *English Courtyard* purchased sub-standard materials. All the wooden frames of the windows and veranda doors have had to be replaced as have most hot water boilers - all at residents' expense.

Why should the residents have to pay for the developers' shortcomings, one might ask? The reason is that all construction was undertaken and financed by *English Courtyard* ***Development*** (ECD) who received the money from the sale of the properties. After two years, ECD assigned the freehold of the whole development to *English Courtyard* ***Association*** (ECA). ECA is a non-profit Housing Association. It has no funds other than the annual fees it receives from the residents. Most of the defects did not come to light during the period before ECA became the owners. ECA failed to undertake a comprehensive survey before accepting the freehold from ECD. Moreover, ECD was defunct by the time that the defects were ascertained. Consequently, neither ECA nor ECD could be called upon to pay for remedial works. Residents were obliged to foot the bill.

My sister Heather, who was widowed in 1992, so liked my *English Courtyard* house that she decided to buy the adjacent property and to move there from her isolated village home in Yorkshire. Unfortunately, she fell and broke her hip in 2004. This left her rather incapacitated. Later she developed chronic short-term memory loss. Nevertheless we remain close friends and see each other nearly every day.

*

When I first started to visit Aldeburgh for the International Music Festivals, I used to stay at Seckford Hall, a fine hotel in a much restored sixteenth century brick building, located on the outskirts of Woodbridge. It was a short drive from the hotel to the concert hall at Snape. I used the hotel for bed and breakfast only. I had my main meals elsewhere. On my third visit to Seckford Hall I was accommodated in a magnificent old bedroom full of oak beams and with an uneven wood floor. But this beautiful room had one big drawback. Underneath was the hotel bar. To come back to this room at, say, 9.45 in the evening, with wonderful music from the concert pulsating through ones mind, only to encounter raucous laughter and gaiety from below was not congenial. On subsequent annual visits to the Festivals, I stayed in one or other of Aldeburgh's hotels.

*

A word or two about the concert hall at Snape. The Maltings at Snape are a group of 19$^{th}$ century brick buildings on the south bank of the River Alde (which, in fact, places them in the parish of Tunstall, not in the parish of Snape). The Alde is tidal as far as the Maltings. To the east are extensive reed beds with distant views of Iken church and – on a fine day – to Aldeburgh, on the skyline.

The main building at the Maltings was converted into a

small concert hall in 1966/67 and became the major venue for the Aldeburgh International Music Festival (see chapter 12). A fire destroyed much of the concert hall soon after it became functional, but it was fully restored in 1969/70 and has been sympathetically enlarged subsequently. The building now houses a restaurant, a separate cafeteria and a small shop. The views from the restaurant and from the cafeteria are stunning. There is a spacious foyer. The concert hall, itself, retains the original brick walls. The acoustics are excellent, especially for chamber music. However, the sound of a large symphony orchestra (which can just be accommodated) is rather overpowering.

When the River Alde reaches the coast just to the south of Aldeburgh, it doesn't flow into the North Sea, but turns sharply south to join the River Ore, some distance down stream. There is an extensive (tidal) estuary at Aldeburgh extending a good way inland from the coast. This is the home of a thriving yacht club.

Aldeburgh also boasts a first class inland golf course and an additional nine-hole course, overlooking the Alde estuary. Shamefully, there is still an aura of out-dated snobbery at the Golf Club, in that there is an artisans' second-class membership, as well as full membership. When a respected member of the community applied for full membership, the Club Committee asked what his profession had been. He had been in the wine trade. The Committee was inclined to deny him full membership until someone said "but he is an Old Etonian". That gave him the entrée!

Aldeburgh town centre still has a distinctly Edwardian flavour, although it has an ancient history, as evidenced by an incongruous 16th century Moot Hall (now a museum). There has been a considerable amount of 20th century housing development, inland from the town centre, but the town's population is still short of 30,000. Many residents are retired middle-class folk, relative newcomers to the town. My GP says people come to Aldeburgh to die and after they have come they forget that – and much else! Aldeburgh is a popular resort for holiday makers, although its shingle beach is not ideal for bathers. There are many "second homes" which lie vacant in the winter months. There are three excellent 3-star hotels, at least two first class restaurants and numerous other venues for wining and dining.

Cultural activities extend well beyond music at Snape and in the town's church and Jubilee Hall. There is a Literary Festival, a Documentary Film Festival, a Drama Festival, a Poetry Festival and numerous thriving clubs in addition to the Golf and Yacht Clubs.

For me, Aldeburgh has one considerable drawback, namely its isolation from London. It no longer has a railway station. Travel to London by rail, in consequence, is not easy. Personally, I always drive to London (also rather burdensome) where I have a club in St. James's Square which has basement parking facilities. When I lived in Maidstone, a day or evening return trip to London was easily accomplished. Now, from Aldeburgh, London visits are much less frequent and normally involve at least one night's stop there.

Aldeburgh has its own micro-climate. It is relatively dry and largely frost-free. The north-east winds are biting and frequently of prolonged duration. But any summer heat is tempered by a cooling sea breeze.

All-in-all, Aldeburgh is a delightful place in which to enjoy one's retirement. I have made many new friends there.

*

I shall now write about my hobbies and leisure pursuits over the years.

Chapter 12

# MUSIC

*Music when soft voices die vibrates in the memory*

Music has been a central preoccupation throughout my life. It merits a chapter of its own.

I have already mentioned in earlier chapters that Lalla had a good voice, that Uncle Douglas was a fine pianist and something of a composer, and that when I was a schoolboy I sang and played the piano. I have also mentioned the Gramophone Society at Dover College, and the fine collection of gramophone records owned by the Master of Selwyn College, Cambridge. Jean had been a talented pianist in her youth. She only just failed the final of her LRAM (Licentiate of the Royal Academy of Music) examination in piano. Sadly, there was never a piano in the various houses in which Jean lived after her marriage. Consequently, her talents were not developed.

When I first arrived at Dover College, the music master was John Stainer – grandson of Sir John Stainer who composed the Easter oratorio called *The Crucifixion.* It was the Stainer grandson who gave me a taste for classical music. Very wisely, it was a gentle introduction: Johann Strauss waltzes, Chopin's piano music and so on. Whether we would have eventually progressed as far as 20th century serial music will never be known. Sadly (it was wartime, remember), Stainer left the College for the armed forces. His replacement was Mrs. Brierley-Garbutt. (I think I have the spelling of her name right). She came to us, I believe, from the Folkestone Symphony Orchestra. She soon concluded, quite rightly, that I would never make much of a pianist. I couldn't play by ear, my sight-reading was poor, and it was a real labour of love to master even simple pieces, such as Schumann's *Scenes from Childhood.* Mrs. Brierley-Garbutt suggested that I should try the violin. A second-hand violin was purchased from a shop in Exeter and I was launched. If I thought the piano hard enough, to play the violin proficiently seemed to me to be completely beyond my limited powers. Violin playing was soon dropped and I struggled on with the piano, at a snail's pace, until eventually, like Jean, I had to abandon it for want of a piano.

There was one excitement with the violin. When I peered inside the instrument, I noticed a printed label saying *Fecit ad Cremona* followed by an eighteenth century date. Did I have a masterpiece? I rushed off to *Phillips* in London for a valuation. *Phillips* said that the instrument was made in the twentieth century, and not earlier. Cleverly, someone had managed to insert the printed note giving an earlier provenance. It was quite untrue! Years later, I gave this violin to my army colleague, David Griffiths. David, unlike me, is a talented violinist. I recently heard him playing the violin at his 50th wedding anniversary.

In the introduction to this book, I said that I have never kept a diary. That is not true in the case of classical music. From the beginning of 1979, I have kept a complete record of all the concerts and recitals that I have attended. I have been lucky in hearing many outstanding artists.

What about the years before 1979? I have a vivid memory of Myra Hess giving a piano recital, during the war, in the National Gallery. Her programme included Bach's *Jesu Joy of Man's Desiring.* It brought a lump to one's throat. I also remember piano recitals in London given by Eileen Joyce and by Benno Moiseiwitsch.

In the army, when I was stationed in Italy I was able to hear a Verdi opera (only one). In Egypt, there were one or two symphony concerts given by talented (and probably professional) German musicians who were prisoners of war. They managed to assemble a full symphony orchestra. How they found all the instruments, heaven alone knows! Probably their repertoire was limited, but I recollect Beethoven being performed.

When I lived in Northern Rhodesia (Zambia), there was

little live music to be had. But I had a reasonable collection of gramophone records, which gave good service.

Peter Katin gave a piano recital in Lusaka. He kept his audience waiting a good 15 – 20 minutes. His excuse was that he had missed a turning on the road north. That caused some amusement. We all knew that there were no turnings off the Great North Road, other than to farms. After playing one or two pieces, Katin asked if there was a piano tuner in the audience. Hilary Quiggin, chairman of the local music society (and Deputy Surveyor General at the time) said, portentously, "I'll see what I can do", and disappeared. More amusement! We all knew that the nearest piano tuner lived some 90 miles away! Quiggin repaired to the hotel bar. The recital continued. The piano was not re-tuned.

There was also a piano recital in Lusaka by one of those pianists who has an extensive repertoire, none of which is played to perfection. She was the sister of a better-known organist called Florence De Jonge. She would ask the audience "what would you like me to play next"? Someone would ask for a fairly well known piece by Chopin or Schubert or whoever. This she promptly proceeded to play, with a moderate degree of competence. After the concert, she was invited to the home of my friends John and Enid Turner for a game of bridge. I was the fourth player. When we made the cut to see who would deal, John, Enid and I each drew a knave. Foolishly, more in jest than in earnest, I said "I bet you £10 that you don't draw the fourth knave." Of course, our pianist did draw the fourth knave. And she held me to my bet. It was quite a lot of money in the 1960s.

D.M. (Mike) Talmage, of whom I have written previously, had been a Major Bandmaster in the army. He staged a number of Gilbert and Sullivan operettas. The least said about them, the better. Hilary Quiggin staged a performance of Handel's *Messiah,* with a few abridgements. His wife, Kay, had an excellent contralto voice. I sang in the choir with the basses.

I feel sure that there must have been one or two concerts in London, whenever I was on long leave. But they have faded from the memory. However, I do remember taking Jean and Aunts Moonie and Beaunes, with their husbands, to a matinée performance of *My Fair Lady,* starring Rex Harrison and Stan Holloway.

I think there were few live concerts for me in England between 1966 and 1979, during Jean's declining years. She was still living with me in Maidstone until shortly before her death in a nursing home in 1979. But by this time, and beyond, I had built up a large collection of long-playing gramophone records (LPs) and there was plenty of broadcast classical music.

Concert going, in earnest, started in 1979. Maidstone, where I then lived, was within easy travelling distance of London. In London, there was – and still is – a veritable cornucopia of concerts, recitals, operas and ballets to be enjoyed. I became a Friend of the London Philharmonic Orchestra, of the Philharmonia Orchestra, of the Royal Opera House and of Wigmore Hall.

An early evening journey to London by car, against the major traffic flow of commuters returning to Kent, and a return journey to Maidstone after a concert, when the roads were relatively quiet, were reasonable propositions. And then, when I was working in London (with SCLSERP/SERPLAN), there were the BBC Monday lunch hour concerts in St. John's, Smith Square, and the occasional evening concert before I returned home to Maidstone.

Not content with what was on offer in London, I started to go to a number of music festivals – Aldeburgh, Bath, Canterbury, City of London, Harrogate, the Leeds International Piano Competition, an early Schubertiad at Hohenhems, the three choirs festival, Salzburg, Wexford (opera) and so on.

At the Canterbury Festival in October 1992, I went to a piano recital by a young British pianist, then calling himself Frederick Kempf. It was clear that he had considerable talent. I asked the woman who was sitting beside me whether she knew anything bout Kempf. She told me that he lived in Kent and had applied to go to the King's School Canterbury. The headmaster asked him if he played rugger. “No”, he replied, “I am a pianist”. The School didn’t take him. I happened to know the headmaster of the King’s School, and asked him about this. He said it was quite true that the school had refused to take Kempf, but the only reason was that he (Kempf) had blotted his copybook at the junior school. Kempf (later calling himself Freddy Kempf) has subsequently had a distinguished career as a pianist. I have heard him playing at the Wigmore Hall and elsewhere.

*

Before leaving Heathrow for the Salzburg Festival one year, I spoke to a woman in our group who was wearing one of those neck collars which are used if one is suffering from whip-lash. Did she want help with her luggage? “Thank you, but no” she replied, “I am being well looked after by the airport”. In Salzburg, the neck collar was promptly discarded and Katie Mien (as she was called) became the life and soul of the party! “How is it that you managed to travel first class” Katie, an Australian, asked me? “I wanted to travel first class, and would have paid. But I was refused”. “It just happened to be the seat I was allocated” I replied. “It didn’t cost me a penny more”. Katie was not best pleased! That is the sort of person she was.

One evening we had nothing on our schedule. I asked our tour leader whether there was anything worth going to. She told me that there was a piano recital by Brendel. “Could you possibly get me a ticket” I asked? Katie’s travelling companion, another Australian woman, chipped in “and one for me, too, please”. More members of our group asked for tickets. In the event, our tour leader was able to get no more than one ticket, which she offered to me, since I was the first in the queue. I told Katie’s Australian friend “I live near London, where Brendel often performs. You live in Australia, and this may be your only chance of hearing him. Do, please take this ticket”. Katie was furious. “Why did you let my friend have the ticket? I wanted it. In any event, she cannot afford it”. On and on Katie ranted. I am sorry to record that the incident resulted in the end of the friendship between the two Australians.

A concert in Salzburg which was on our schedule was a performance of Beethoven's double concerto, to be performed by Anne Sophie Mutter and Rostropovich. It was common knowledge that Rostropovich was having an affair with the beautiful Anne Sophie. Galina Vishnevskaya, Rostropovich's wife, refused to let him travel to Salzburg unless she (Galina) accompanied him. Rostropovich didn't come! Anne Sophie had to change the programme and play two Mozart Violin Concerti instead.

On another evening there was a semi-staged performance of Franz Schmidt's oratorio *Das Buch mit Sieben Siegeln* (The Book with Seven Seals) performed in Salzburg cathedral. At the opening performance, there had been a certain amount of nudity in the cast. The Archbishop objected. On the evening we went, many protesters had gathered outside the Cathedral, condemning the Archbishop for being narrow-minded. It was touch and go whether we would hear the oratorio. Fortunately, we did. All the singers were fully clothed!

*

I attended the Spring Festival in Prague in 1988. It seemed to me that Prague was one of the most beautiful cities in the world. There was St. Vitus's Cathedral, with its casket containing the remains of "Good" King Wenceslas, the Hardçany Citadel, and the Charles IV Bridge over the River Vltava. Czechoslovakia was still under communist control in 1988. At the opening Festival concert, the communist hierarchy arrived at the concert hall – no wives – and sat in a prominent box. A communist anthem was played. Many of the Czechs remained seated. We then heard the full version of Smetana's *Ma Vlast.*

Our tour leader was a Czech who had defected to the west and who had an architectural practice in London. He asked if we would mind if he took a day off so that he could visit his sister in a nearby town. Of course, he could, we said. His sister worked in a public library. The library had books on such subjects as aeronautics and military history. They were classified by the regime as *secret*. Consequently, the poor girl was unable to get a passport and couldn't leave the country.

The Czech citizens were most friendly. Those who did have passports were often unable to afford the costs of travelling abroad. They hoped that a kindly tourist from the west would perhaps invite them as guests, so that they could save hotel bills.

There were plenty of first class musical performances during the Festival, and the Dvorak Museum to visit. One afternoon, we were able to get seats for Smetana's *Bartered Bride.* It was not on our schedule. We sat in the very back row of the "gods" in the opera house. In common with opera houses worldwide, the programme told one how many previous performances there had been, of that production. I forget the exact number, but I believe it was well into the tens of thousands! It looked as though the stage scenery was the original! Nevertheless, it was a delightful afternoon.

I got to know Fred and Dorothy Brittenden in Prague. They are avid concert goers whom I often met later at London musical venues. Sadly, Dorothy died at the end of 2012.

*

Later in 1988, I went to the Verona Opera Festival. Our group stayed in a very comfortable hotel, with a swimming pool, at Pescatina, some distance outside Verona. It was a great experience to be seated for the opera inside the majestic Roman coliseum. But, in my view, the performances suffered from being staged in such a vast arena. The orchestra, instead of being closely grouped in its various sections, was strung out from one end of the platform to the other. When an aria was sung, the artist would take centre stage, forget about any acting and sing at full throttle so as to be heard in the gods. The Italians in the audience were uninhibitedly critical. One poor tenor received so many boos at the end of Act 1 of an opera, that he was replaced by his understudy for the remainder of the programme.

I made friends with a widow who had a job at a Roman Catholic boys' boarding school in England. As far as I was concerned, our friendship was purely platonic. But I think the widow hoped it might develop into something more profound.

But, as I have already said, once I feel chased, the drawbridge is withdrawn.

*

The following year (1989), I went on a "musical" cruise on the River Danube, from Passau to Bucharest. As well as concerts on shore at Salzburg, Vienna and Bucharest, there were evening performances on board, given by the Duke Quartet, who travelled on our boat with us. Unfortunately for me, the Quartet had the cabins next to mine, where they practised assiduously. Our "musical" tour leader was a lecturer called Joan Kemp-Potter. She fell in my estimation when she asserted that Vivaldi's *Four Seasons* was a concerto in 4 movements which wouldn't last long. I had to tell an elderly lady in our party who had asked about this, that in fact *The Four Seasons* comprised 4 separate violin concerti – one for each season of the year.

William Blezard, Joan Kemp-Potter's husband travelled with us. He had been Joyce Grenfell's accompanist. He was great fun. He played as best he could on the terrible on-board piano and composed amusing musical ditties for us.

As well as the British party on board, there were tourist groups from Germany and from the United States. The latter behaved most discourteously. They chatted, drank and smoked during the performances of classical music by the Duke Quartet.

*Serenissima* was an up-market travel agency founded by John Julius Norwich (Viscount Norwich). He named his agency after the sobriquet for Venice – *La Serenissima.* Norwich was an ardent conservationist of Venice and had written a two-volume history of the city. I travelled with *Serenissima* twice; once to Russia, which I shall relate in chapter 15, and the second time to a *Schubertiade* in Austria.

We were a small group of Schubert fans in Austria. We enjoyed each other's company and some wonderful Schubert recitals at Hohenems. Highlights were performances in the open courtyard of Hohenems Palace, but one evening it rained. We kept dry under a canvas awning, but rain on canvas is not silent! We saw Lord Norwich at the *Schubertiade*, but he avoided his paying customers. I became a close friend of one couple at the *Schubertiade* – Stanley and Anne Klar.

Stanley Klar is an avid opera buff. He had seen scores of operas, year after year. He whetted my appetite for opera at Wexford in Eire. Another couple I got to know at the *Schubertiade* were the Bosanquets of Alnwick. Jay Bosanquet became a useful contact when I came to writing a biography of Sir Thomas Sutherland (see next chapter).

*

When I went to the first of my two Wexford Opera Festivals, in 1990, I flew to Cork and hired a car. The drive to *White's Hotel* in Wexford took longer than I had anticipated. On the journey, the heavens opened. I was obliged to stop at a garage to find how to work the windscreen wipers. Eventually in Wexford, it was difficult finding parking at or near *White's Hotel*. The end result was that I booked into the hotel too late for an evening meal before the opera and too late to change into my dinner jacket (*de rigueur* at the opera). I just managed to get to the little theatre in time for the opening bars of Nicholas Maw's *The Rising of the Moon*. Fortunately, no-one said "go back and dress properly"! It was the start of the season. In the morning after a performance, one could freely join in discussions with the artists and music critics over coffee in the hotel.

The second time I went to the Wexford Festival, in 2003, the party I was with flew to Dublin, took a coach to Wexford and stayed in the newly-revamped *Talbot's Hotel*. It was not quite the same fun.

I have been fortunate to have seen opera not only in Italy (on two different occasions) and at Wexford, but also in Cardiff, Edinburgh, Glyndebourne, Prague, St. Petersburg, Snape Maltings, Sydney and, of course, London. I was a regular visitor to the London Coliseum, where I met Nicky (see later), but after a while I gave that venue up because every opera was sung in English translation which seemed not to meld with the musical score. Moreover, diction of the principal singers was far from perfect and many of the productions I judged to be "too clever by half". The Royal Opera House at Covent Garden was (and still is) my favourite venue for opera and ballet. Productions invariably are superb. In recent years I have been to live relays of opera from the Metropolitan, New York. They are relayed to our local cinema screen in Aldeburgh. It is not as thrilling as attending live performances, but much cheaper!

Our local cinema has now started to screen live performances of the *Bolshoi Ballet.* I have also seen ballet in St. Petersburg, Moscow, Snape Maltings and in several London venues. On one occasion at the Royal Opera House in Covent Garden, I was privileged to meet Dame Ninette de Valois in the crush bar.

*

For many years I went to the June Festivals in Aldeburgh. Today I live in Aldeburgh, as I have related in the previous chapter. Benjamin Britten, Peter Pears and Imogen Holst are buried side by side in Aldeburgh Church graveyard, only a few hundred metres from my home. Aldeburgh church boasts a fine memorial window to Benjamin Britten, designed by John Piper. Piper's wife Myfanwy worked on some of the libretti of Britten's operas. Recently a modern sculpture by Maggy Hamblin, in memory of Britten, was (controversially) erected on the open beach between Aldeburgh and Thorpeness. In my opinion it is aesthetically pleasing, but inappropriately sited. It has been vandalised on several occasions,

Most importantly, the Maltings at Snape, which Britten and Pears converted into an acoustically-perfect concert hall, continues to flourish and is the venue for many fine concerts. Alongside the Maltings, is a school founded by Britten and Pears for advanced studies by young musical students. A strong link with Britten is maintained in that the composer's nephew, Alan Britten is chairman of The Friends of Aldeburgh Music. Alan and his wife come to most of, if not all the concerts at the Festivals. Local churches are used as venues for a number of recitals.

Perhaps the artists who now come to perform at the Maltings are not quite the same top-notchers whom Britten and Pears could attract when they were alive. Nevertheless, the standard of performances continues to be high, as is underlined by the fact that many concerts are recorded for later transmission by BBC Radio 3.

Understandably, one hears a lot of Britten's compositions at the Maltings. Before I started going to the Aldeburgh Festivals, I wrote:

Bach, Beethoven, Brahms
I welcome with open arms.
But I'm not so smitten
With Benjamin Britten –
A bit of a "b" with his charms.

Now I have grown to appreciate Britten's music far more, especially his operas and the songs he composed.

*

During the Aldeburgh Festival in June each year, it is customary to stage a couple of walks. These are gentle affairs: a coach ride to a suitable starting point, an amble for perhaps an hour and a half, a light lunch, another amble for an hour or so and finally a return to Aldeburgh by coach.

I went on one such walk in 1992. A picnic box was provided for our lunch break. I was finishing my sandwiches when a young man came up to me and asked if there was any rubbish to be cleared away. He was a Hesse student. I should explain that during the Aldeburgh Festivals, young students are given simple tasks helping the organisers, in return for which they are able to go to concerts without paying, and they can live cheaply. The students also stage impromptu concerts for the entertainment of concert goers.

The young student who came to collect my rubbish after the picnic was Richard Whalley. We chatted for a while. I next saw him on duty collecting tickets on the coach that plied between Aldeburgh and the Maltings at Snape. Richard suggested that I should come to the students' concert to be given in Aldeburgh

Church. He would be playing the piano, both as soloist and as accompanist.

So began an important and enduring friendship. Richard and I went to a few London concerts together. He came and stayed with me in Maidstone. I met his parents. Richard obtained a good music degree at York University, followed by a scholarship to Harvard. Later he got his Doctor of Philosophy degree from Harvard. His heart and soul are in composition, but teaching brings in the bread and butter. Richard is now married (to an American). They have two children and live in Manchester where Richard teaches composition at the university.

I think it was on the walk when I first met Richard that I was walking beside an elderly man who told me that he lived in Aldeburgh. I asked him whether he had known Britten and Pears socially. He said that Britten didn't mix much with the locals; Pears was rather more gregarious. On one occasion Pears was his dinner party guest. Pears noticed that there were some birthday cards on the mantelpiece. When the dinner came to a close, Pears said "I expect you know that our hostess has recently celebrated her birthday. I should like to sing her a small song, if I may". The world-celebrated tenor then proceeded to sing *Happy Birthday to You!*

*

I made several important new friends as a direct result of meeting people at musical events. I must mention three young men, in particular.

First was Nicky Elbercht. At the time, Nicky was working as a barman at the London Coliseum for English National Opera. (He told me that in the course of one evening at the opera, Denis Thatcher had drunk 10 double gin-and-its)! When I first spoke to him, Nicky told me he was interested in music, so I gave him a ticket to a concert at the Royal Festival Hall. Next time I saw Nicky at the Coliseum, he said he was disappointed not to find me at that concert, too. After that, there were numerous occasions when we went to concerts together. On one or two occasions, Nicky spent a weekend with me in Maidstone. He was a delightful companion.

Shortly after we became friendly, Nicky gave me a farewell kiss when we parted company after a concert. I was completely taken by surprise. It was only the second male-to-male kiss that I had experienced. (I have recounted the first occasion in chapter 5). To Nicky it probably meant nothing. He was continental! He had a Dutch father and a Swedish mother (separated). But for me, it was the beginning of a deep and sincere affection. Nothing untoward between us occurred and eventually, to my sorrow, Nicky chose to drop out of my life. I wish him well wherever he may now be.

The second encounter, which I shall now describe, proved to be of the utmost importance to both of us. David Bartram has become my best friend. It is a friendship that I know will endure until the day I die. I look upon David as a son. He is the executor of, and principal beneficiary under my Will.

On 7 March 1991 (we both remember the date!), I was sitting reading a book, waiting to enter the auditorium of the Royal Festival Hall, when a young man asked whether anyone was sitting in the chair beside me. "No. Do sit down", I said. He introduced himself as David Belcher (later he changed his surname to Bartram). David was thrilled to have got the last ticket for the evening's performance of Brahms's 1st Piano Concerto and 1st Symphony. His seat was behind the orchestra: mine was in the stalls, facing the orchestra. We waved to one another after we had sat down. In the interval, I returned to the place where I had been sitting before the concert began. Along came David. We chatted again and presumably exchanged addresses and telephone numbers. So started a very special relationship between two music lovers. David was 20. He was reading history at the Royal Holloway College. For his 21st birthday, I gave him tickets for two people for a short Philharmonia Orchestra series. David invited me to join him for one of these concerts.

David and I have since gone to many concerts together. We have written to one another nearly every week. David got his degree, went to Sidney Sussex College, Cambridge for a teacher training course, and has been happily teaching at state schools ever since. As I write this, David is the Deputy Headmaster of a state school and is living in Norfolk with a wife, two young sons and an adopted daught. We meet fairly frequently.

David and I celebrated the 20th anniversary of our first meeting with lunch and a concert in the Festival Hall. We were joined by Valeriy Sokolov (of whom more later) who was about to play the Tchaikovsky violin concerto with the Philharmonia Orchestra.

The third important friendship was with Bodo Goerisch. I met Bodo when he was working at the Wigmore Hall. He is an exceptionally good-looking and charismatic young man, of German descent. He was determined to get a job as a model. He invited me to look at a portfolio of his pictures which he had prepared for a model agency. They were stunning. I asked Bodo if he would like to see an exhibition of pictures at the Royal Academy. "Thank you", he said. But he failed to turn up! Excuses followed. I wondered if he had a drugs problem and I made enquiries as to how one should go about helping him. It turned out that he was, indeed, taking drugs, but they were drugs prescribed by a doctor for treatment of the depression which periodically afflicts him. So began another remarkable friendship between two people of such dissimilar age and background. We saw quite a lot of each other, and Bodo came to stay with me at Maidstone. Unfortunately, Bodo failed to make his mark with a London model agency. He decided to try his luck in the United States. I helped him with his passage money.

In the States, Bodo has failed again to make the break through which I believe he merited. After a few ups and downs and further bouts of depression, I fear that Bodo is no further forward in the US than he was in the UK. But he intends to stick it out there. Bodo is gay. He has had two long-term boy-friends in the States, both of whom I have met. I believe the second one, William, will become a life-long partner. No doubt because he is gay (and continental, to boot), Bodo expresses his affection for me with hugs and kisses. I am happy to respond in like fashion, but that is as far as it goes!

Bodo (like David) comes from a broken home. By all accounts, Bodo's father, who has since died, was a brute – to his wife and to his children. Perhaps Bodo looks upon me as a substitute father figure. Certainly, I worry about him and his future as though he were my son (in addition to David). I have tried to help him as best I can. I have made sure that Bodo and David have met. I am pleased to say that they get on well together.

*

I first met Valeriy Sokolov at a concert in the Wigmore Hall. We were sitting beside one another. Janáček's string quartets were being played. Valeriy was closely studying the scores. He had what was clearly a violin case with him. I asked him if he was a musical student. "Yes" he said "I am studying violin at the Royal College of Music". "And where is your home" I asked? "I come from the Ukraine" Valeriy said.

When I got home I found I had an old biography of Janáček. I rang the Royal College of Music and said that I had met a violin student of the College who came from the Ukraine. I didn't know his name, but I should like to let him have a biography of Janáček. If I posted the book to the College, would they pass it on for me? The College readily agreed. The book was sent. For several weeks I heard nothing. Then I had a charming letter from Valeriy together with a DVD of him playing the violin. The DVD was entitled *Natural Born Fiddler.* I was non-plussed! Valeriy was already a star – and not yet aged 21. So began a close friendship between the two of us.

Valeriy came to stay with me in Aldeburgh one weekend, early in our friendship. I showed him all the sites associated with Benjamin Britten. After practising assiduously on his violin one morning, Valeriy said "I should like to play something especially for you. What would you like"? I said "it is an Elgar centenary, Perhaps you would like to play something by him". Valeriy then played *Salut d'Amour*. It brought a tear to my eye.

Valeriy now lives in Munich, but frequently performs in this country and elsewhere, world-wide. I go to his British performances if I can.

*

Since 2004, I have been annually to chamber music weekends at the *Castle Hotel*, Taunton. Each weekend there are four recitals in the hotel, the first on Friday evening, two more on Saturday and the fourth on Sunday morning. The musicians dine with us on the Friday and Saturday evenings. Each recital is preceded by a half hour talk by a well respected musicologist. The *Castle Hotel* is a comfortable family-run hotel. The father of the present owner was an Old Dovorian, as was his uncle who was the Manager of the *Imperial Hotel*, Torquay, in its hey-day.

Coincidentally, the family-run hotel in Aldeburgh, the *Wentworth*, is managed by an Old Dovorian. The *Wentworth* is my luncheon venue on Fridays in the winter months, after the midday concerts given in Aldeburgh by young musicians studying at the Snape Maltings.

*

When I moved from Maidstone to Aldeburgh, I disposed of my large collection of LPs, but I kept many tapes, all of which I later jettisoned. Now I have a considerable collection of CDs. I can therefore still enjoy plenty of recorded music

There are also several live musical events close to Aldeburgh/Snape Maltings, which I patronise regularly. They include: orchestral concerts in Westleton Church; and chamber music recitals in St Mary's Church, Woodbridge, in Cratfield Church, in a recording studio at Potton Hall and, until recently, in Blackthorpe Barn outside Bury St Edmunds. That so many live concerts are readily available compensates, in some measure, for the loss of the concerts I enjoyed so frequently in London.

61. Nicky Elbercht

62. Bodo Goerisch

63. David Bartram

64. The Author with Bodo Goerisch & David Bartram in Cambridge

65. Richard Whalley

66. Valeriy Sokolov

Chapter13

# PUBLICATIONS

As editor of my school magazine (*The Dovorian*), my editorials reached a limited public (as did a few poems which I wrote for the magazine). One of those editorials was, in fact, published in *The Kent Messenger.* But I hardly regard these efforts as "publications" in its generally accepted sense.

Neither do I regard as "the real thing" the twenty or so articles which I have written for the Clan Sutherland Society Newsletter since 1994. (Perhaps the Society Newsletter is short of copy)! An article in *The Journal of the Scottish Military Historical Society* and a letter to *The Times* likewise hardly qualify as publications. But I have had three books published, and another already completed, which I hope to have published. Moreover this autobiography will be freely distributed, if not actually published.

My first book to be published was entitled *A Fighting Clan.* Its subtitle was *Sutherland Officers 1250-1850.* In addition to an opening narrative, highlighting the contribution to history made by officers called Sutherland, the book goes on to give full details of the careers of all those officers, both naval and military, who saw service between 1250 and 1850.

*John Donald*, a reputable and long-established firm of publishers in Scotland agreed to publish *A Fighting Clan.* But it was at a time of economic recession, and they withdrew their offer. Leo Cooper (the husband of the author Jilly Cooper), who publishes military books, recommended a newly-established publisher called *Avon Books. Avon Books* offered to publish *A Fighting Clan* on the basis of the costs being shared by themselves and the author. I decided to go ahead. Sadly, *Avon Books* proved to be totally incompetent, both as printers and as publishers. I wrote to Leo Cooper suggesting that he refrained from recommending *Avon Books* to any other aspiring author. I was not surprised when, shortly after my book was printed, *Avon Books* went bankrupt, leaving a warehouse full of books, including several hundred copies of *A Fighting Clan*, to be pulped. I lost most of my investment.

*

Many people will have seen the film *Gosford Park.* Few may know that the correct name of the house and estate for the setting of the film is *Wrotham Park.* Wrotham Park lies within the Metropolitan Green Belt, between High Barnet and Potters Bar. It is the seat of Julian Byng It has been my good fortune to have been entertained to lunch twice at Wrotham Park. How did that come about?

When I was researching the Sutherland family history in India (see chapter 1), I noticed that a certain Andrew George Colebrooke Sutherland was a grandson of Louisa Colebrooke, daughter of Sir George Colebrooke Bart. I became interested in the Colebrooke family.

For two generations, the Colebrookes had owned Chilham Castle in Kent. Numerous Colebrookes were interred in a crypt in Chilham Church. I wrote a series of four articles, tracing the history of the family, which I thought might be published, one day, in the *Kent Messenger.* Then I thought of conflating the four articles and having them printed as a book. I sought the advice of a dear friend (Jane Moore) who had worked for *Murrays,* the well-known London publishers. Jane read the articles and expressed the opinion that I would not find a publisher.

There the matter rested until David Muspratt, a friend of mine, urged me once again to turn the four articles into a book and have it printed. I told David about the advice which I had had from Jane. I also told David that I knew many Colebrookes had had their portraits painted, some by Joshua Reynolds. The De Witt Library in London knew all about these portraits, but wouldn't disclose who owned them. It was essential, in my view, to illustrate any publication with photographs of these portraits. After some difficulty, I checked with Lord Massereene and

Ferrard, the then owner of Chilham Castle, that there were no Colebrooke portraits hanging on his castle walls.

A month or two later, David Muspratt wrote to say that he had been rummaging through some papers in a trunk in his attic, when he came across a letter addressed to his mother, Lady Muspratt from Lady Strafford saying, in effect, "do come round and see the Colebrooke portraits, which I know are of interest to you".

I tracked down the current (8th) Earl of Strafford, but thought it unlikely that he had the Colebrooke portraits because his address was Apple Tree Cottage! Nevertheless, I wrote to him. He replied saying that his cousin Julian Byng had the portraits at Wrotham Park.

I then wrote to Julian Byng. Byng invited me to lunch. I arrived punctually at the grand wrought iron, locked gates at the entrance to Wrotham Park, rang the house and announced who I was. The entrance gates swung open and I drove up a long drive to this rather austere looking eighteenth century house. A butler appeared, opened my car door, showed me into the drawing room and offered me a drink. Byng then appeared and immediately put me at ease by inviting me to call him Julian and asking me if he could call me Malcolm. "I'm sorry my son is not here to meet you", he said. "He is over in France getting our aeroplane repaired. And my wife is with Molly Salisbury, organising a flag day". I had noticed a pair of binoculars and a race card on a table in the entrance hall: "We had to go to Ascot in the helicopter" said Julian.

We were sipping our glasses of sherry when Lady Longman was ushered in. "Where is everybody" she enquired? "My dear Elizabeth" said Julian "the party is tomorrow". Lady Longman's diary was produced and consulted. The diary was correct: Lady Longman was mistaken. "Oh, dear! I'll motor on to London and see you tomorrow". Julian rang for the butler. "Will it be alright if Lady Longman stays to have lunch with us"? "Certainly, Sir"!

After a short interval, a delicious lunch was served. There

was no evidence that a third person had to be served at very short notice. I couldn't but wonder whether the butler got a decent lunch himself.

After lunch, Julian showed me the Colebrooke portraits hanging on his walls alongside those of many other ancestors. It was a fine collection. One of the portraits was of Admiral Sir John Byng for whom Wrotham Park was built. The Admiral was court martialled and sentenced to death in 1757, for the loss of Menorca. His execution by firing squad on the quarterdeck of *HMS Monarque* prompted Voltaire's famous quip *pour encourager les autres*!

After studying my manuscript, Julian agreed that it ought to be published as a book, illustrated with the Colebrooke portraits. He generously offered to pay for all the costs. I was invited to find a printer.

I approached Alison Weir, a Kent County Councillor, who had a small printing press at Sittingbourne. She gave Julian a quotation, which he accepted. Work started.

Rather portentously and sarcastically, I entitled the book *Sola Bona Quae Honesta,* which was the Colebrooke family motto. This translates as "those things only are good, which are honest". Over the centuries, the Colebrooke family fortunes waxed and waned and waxed again, not always with the highest probity!

While printing the book, Alison Weir noticed an article in a woman's magazine about a firm of caterers called *Alisons* – her name. So she read it and sent it to me. *Alisons* said the biggest job that they had ever undertaken was for Byng. They had to engage 60 chefs to cater for a party of some 1,000 guests at Wrotham Park. Some guests stayed on for breakfast next morning. Alison Weir's wry comment was: "I wish I had read this before submitting my quotation"!

I was invited to a second luncheon at Wrotham Park. This time Julian's wife, son and secretary joined us. Five of us sat down to the meal. We were waited on by two male servants. Julian's son said to his father "you know so much about all the people whose portraits we have. This should be recorded, too. Malcolm should write another book about the Byngs". Julian said nothing: neither did I, although I would dearly have loved such a commission.

In the course of our discussions, Julian told me how it was that he was related to the Colebrookes. Edmund Henry Byng, the 6th Earl of Strafford (1862-1971) had married (in 1894) a daughter of Sir Thomas Edward Colebrooke (1813-1890). They had two daughters, but no son. The elder daughter (Florence) Elizabeth was Julian's mother. Her marriage had broken down before Julian was born. Julian took her surname as his own surname, rather than have his father's surname. His father was a man called Michael Lafone.

What I now write may be unknown to Julian. I sincerely hope it will not offend him or his family.

*

Mopani is a small tree which grows in areas of low rainfall in central and southern Africa. It was the nickname given to a man called Clarke who owned the Zambezi sawmills in Livingstone in the early 20th century. Mopani Clarke had a beautiful daughter called Erica. She was irresistible to men.

Erica's first husband was Sir William Fitzgerald QC. Sir William was then the Attorney General of Northern Rhodesia. Later he held a similar appointment in Palestine. I was destined to meet William and Erica's son, Michael Fitzgerald QC. It was Michael Fitzgerald who represented the Government at the Select Committee hearing on the Channel Tunnel Bill (see chapter 10). I, it will be recalled, attended all the meetings of the Select Committee. Consequently, I got to know Michael Fitzgerald quite well. But I have to record that once he knew that I had met his mother (the beautiful Erica), there was no further converse between us!

Sir William Fitzgerald divorced Erica. She then married Michael Lafone, who was Julian Byng's father by a previous marriage. Michael and Erica were living in Lusaka, when I myself was living there. I didn't meet them, but I knew they were the subject of a great scandal. One evening at the Lusaka Club, so it was said, Erica discovered that Michael was having an affair with an African woman. She went home, got the riding crop out of the cupboard, returned to the Club and gave Michael a public horse-whipping. That was the end of Erica's second marriage.

Erica's third, and as far as I know, last husband was Colonel Critchley. Critchley had two attractive daughters from a previous marriage. I believe he came to Northern Rhodesia from Kenya. The Critchleys ran a country club (called *The Blue Lagoon*) a few miles south of Lusaka. It was popular. It had good food, a swimming pool and, of course, the two beautiful daughters. It was at the Blue Lagoon where I met Erica, Michael Fitzgerald's mother; although only briefly.

*

To revert to my book *Sola Bona Quae Honesta,* Julian asked me to draw up a list of people whom I considered should receive complimentary copies. I included the Earl of Strafford on the list. It was he, in effect, who had set the ball rolling. I think that Strafford was the only name which Julian struck off my list. I make no comment! I received only two complimentary copies, myself. I had to **buy** a third copy to give to a friend who was not on my list!

*

Over the past few years, I have been working, off and on, on the supplement to *A Fighting Clan*, which I have entitled *And On They Fought*. For this book I have researched all Sutherland officers who served between 1851 and 1950. It was no mean task. First, the period includes the two World Wars, during both of which there was conscription. That factor alone swelled the number of Sutherland officers. Secondly, the Clan had multiplied and dispersed. Consequently, my researches had to take account of Sutherland officers who had served in the armed forces of Australia, Canada, New Zealand and the United States. Of necessity, since there were so many Sutherland officers, the resulting book is selective. It is not comprehensive, as is *A*

*Fighting Clan*. Even so, it is considerably lengthier. I have yet to find a publisher.

*

At a local club dinner in Aldeburgh one evening, I introduced myself to the lady sitting on my right. She was Marona Creighton. When she heard that my surname was *Sutherland*, she asked me if I was related to her great uncle Sir Thomas Sutherland. "No" I replied, "but I know a little bit about him and that he had two sons who became army officers". This exchange eventually led to my being invited to write a biography of Sir Thomas Sutherland. After some initial research, I accepted Mr & Mrs Creightons' invitation, on the strict understanding that the Creightons, not I, would see to the printing and publication of the book.

Sir Thomas was a remarkable man who lived from 1834 to 1922. He was the Chairman and Managing Director of P & O for many years; he founded HSBC while he was serving with P & O in Hong Kong; he persuaded Disraeli to get the British government to purchase a controlling interest in the *Suez Canal Company*, of which he was a Deputy Chairman; he was a Member of Parliament for Greenock for several years, and he was appointed GCMG. A substantial outline of his career is given in the *Dictionary of National Biography*, but I thought that Sir Thomas deserved a fuller biography.

Writing a fuller biography was made difficult because very few of Sir Thomas's private papers and photographs had survived. I had to rely almost entirely on published material. The end result was a short biography of some 30,000 words only.

I was fortunate in tracking down a few Sutherland papers which had found their way into the Tate Gallery Archives. This came about because Sir Thomas's daughter, Helen Sutherland inherited her father's papers, and when Helen died those papers which she had kept were inherited by her life-long friend Nicolete Gray. Helen Sutherland and Nicolete Gray were luminaries in the art world.

After Helen's death, Nicolete arranged an exhibition of paintings which had been owned by Helen. In the exhibition catalogue Nicolete mentioned that Helen had been a friend of the Bosanquet family in Northumberland. I recalled that I had met Jay Bosanquet (see chapter 12). I wrote to Jay and asked him what he knew of Helen Sutherland and Nicolete Gray. Jay gave me an anecdote and the address of Nicolete's son. The son referred me to his sister Sophy Gray. Sophy supplied me with copies of the scant remains of the Sutherland family papers which her mother had inherited and which were lodged with the Tate Gallery Archives after her mother's death

In the event, the Thomas Sutherland biography was printed and published privately at my own expense, not by the Creightons, but with financial help from them and from HSBC. P&O, the shipping company for which Sir Thomas had done so much, offered no help, not even to the extent of stocking copies of the book for sale in the shops on their cruise ships.

*

*When once the itch of literature comes over a man, nothing can cure it but the scratching of a pen.*

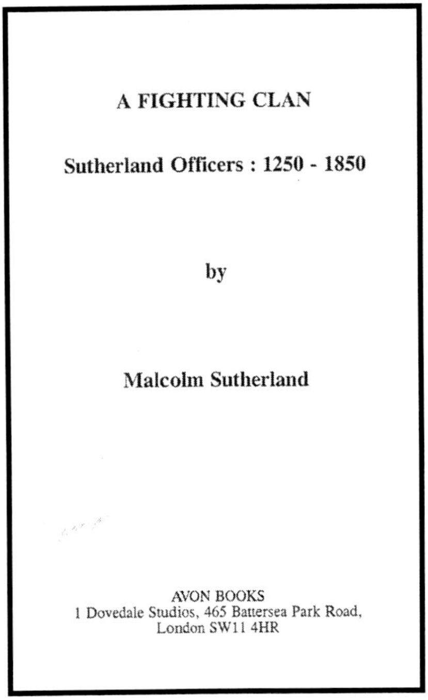

A FIGHTING CLAN

Sutherland Officers : 1250 - 1850

by

Malcolm Sutherland

AVON BOOKS
1 Dovedale Studios, 465 Battersea Park Road,
London SW11 4HR

67. A Fighting Clan – Title Page

68. Sola Bona Quae Honesta – Dust Jacket

69. Wrotham Park (Gosford)

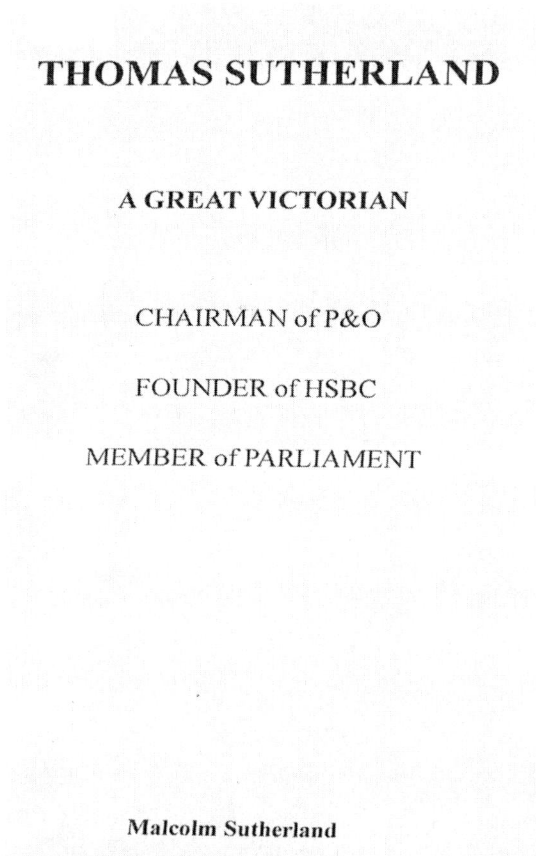

# THOMAS SUTHERLAND

**A GREAT VICTORIAN**

CHAIRMAN of P&O

FOUNDER of HSBC

MEMBER of PARLIAMENT

**Malcolm Sutherland**

70. Thomas Sutherland – Title Page

71. Biography of Sir Thomas Sutherland – Illustrations on flyer

Chapter 14

# TRAVEL

*Much have I travell'd in the realms of gold,*
*And many good and stately kingdoms seen.*

Travel had been a feature in both my military and colonial careers. When I was in the Sappers I saw much of Egypt, Italy and Palestine and, more briefly, I saw something of France, Malta, Saudi Arabia and Transjordan. When I was in the Colonial (later Overseas Civil) Service, I saw much of Northern Rhodesia (Zambia), Southern Rhodesia (Zimbabwe) and South Africa and, more briefly, France (again), Greece, Madeira, Norway, Portuguese East Africa and Switzerland. Some of these travels have been recorded in earlier chapters, as have many travels associated with my passion for classical music. In this chapter I will recount some other travels.

*

Scotland has always been a favoured holiday destination. Although the Scottish blood flowing in my veins has been diluted over succeeding generations, with a father called Sutherland and a mother called McJannet I have naturally been interested in my Scottish roots. Genealogical research has taken me to the county of Sutherland whence my Sutherland ancestors came, and to Ayrshire whence my McJannet ancestors came. I have also visited Edinburgh for genealogical research in the General Register Office, the National Library and the Scottish Genealogical Society.

I was a teenager when I first visited Scotland. Aunt Moonie's husband, who was then an officer in the RAF, was stationed in Fifeshire for a while. They had a flat at Lundin Links and they invited me to stay with them for a few days, one summer. Scattered memories of this occasion include stealing strawberries from the larder, playing golf on the seaside links, and acting as their barman at a cocktail party given by my aunt and uncle. I was reprimanded for pinching the strawberries, but congratulated on my skills as a barman when my uncle discovered next morning that one bottle of gin hadn't been opened! My early aptitude at golf was never matched in later life, as I have already recorded.

My next visit to Scotland happened during one of my long leaves from Africa. My mother was with me. We motored to Crianlarich in Stirling, an ideal location for further day trips by car. Staying in the hotel was an elderly man called Macdonald. He had been a Crown Court Recorder in Hull. Macdonald was attired in full Highland evening dress for dinner every night – a glorious spectacle! I asked him "have the Macdonalds and the Campbells now buried the hatchet"? (It was centuries after the massacre of Glencoe). "Not a bit of it" Macdonald replied. "Today I had lunch at the *Loch Awe Hotel.* They have carpeted the public rooms with tartan carpets. I don't approve, but it gave me great delight to tramp up and down on a Campbell tartan carpet".

*

Many years later, after my mother's death, I had a solo motoring trip to the north of Scotland. My headquarters was the *Sutherland Arms Hotel* in Golspie. The weather was kind and I saw the habitat of my Sutherland ancestors. Beautiful scenery didn't compensate for a generally harsh climate, with infertile land and virtually no industry. It was small wonder my Sutherland great-great- grandfather left Scotland for good.

I think it was on another occasion that I travelled around Ayrshire, the McJannet ancestral home. Lowland Ayrshire may not be as beautiful as the Sutherland Highlands, but it is more fertile and more populous. Perhaps it was the paucity of employment opportunities that persuaded my McJannet great-grandfather John McJannet (1823-1875) and his elder brother William (1821-1881) to migrate to Norfolk. I discovered the grave of their father Thomas (1792-1854) in the churchyard at Dalrymple. In the 1852 Census, Thomas was described as a land steward.

*

On one memorable occasion, Heather and I took the train to Edinburgh where we boarded the *Royal Scotsman* for a 4-day journey north to Mallaig and back. The train was equipped with small en-suite cabins, such as one would find on a cruise ship. There was an observation car and two restaurant cars. At night, the train would halt at a siding so that sleep was undisturbed. There were several day stops for visits to places of interest. The food served on the train was first class. A fellow passenger, who owned a restaurant in Yorkshire, said he would employ one of the two chefs on the train, simply on the basis of the excellence of a soufflé which had been served one evening.

*

I have attended the Edinburgh International Music Festival on several occasions. On one visit I stayed in a small boarding house some way from the city centre. The city centre was easily reached by bus. Evening concerts and morning genealogical research were the order of the day.

I had booked and paid a deposit for a few nights stay in the same boarding house for the following year. But in the interval the boarding house had changed hands and the new owner had no knowledge of my booking, nor of my deposit. I discovered this only the day before I was due to arrive in Edinburgh, with a sheaf of pre-paid concert tickets in my hand. The new owner of the boarding house could not put me up and despite considerable search I was unable to secure a room elsewhere. Accordingly, the whole trip to Edinburgh was aborted. After a prolonged struggle and eventual recourse to the Small Claims Court, I managed to recoup most of my original outlay.

My London Club (the Army & Navy) has reciprocal arrangements with some of the Edinburgh Clubs, including the Royal Scots Club and the New Club. One year at festival time in Edinburgh, I stayed at the New Club, which (like my London Club) has the benefit of on-site private parking. I came down to breakfast on the first morning wearing a tie and a buttoned-up cardigan. I was curtly invited to return to the dining room wearing a jacket!

Heather and I stayed in the Royal Scots one year, at festival time. Although I had my own car, we decided to go to the opera one night by taxi: parking in the vicinity of the new opera house was difficult. Heather asked the taxi driver if he would kindly pick us up at the end of the opera. "No", he replied. "I shall be at home with my wife by then". Heather tried to soft-soap him by saying that we were *Sutherlands*. "Sutherlands" he said? "Cattle thieves". Heather then said "our mother was a *McJannet*". "More cattle thieves" came back the retort. So when the opera was over, we tried, without success, to find another taxi. It was pouring with rain and we got soaked standing in a queue at a bus stop. Eventually we caught a bus, but we transferred to a taxi half-way back to the Royal Scots. We were wet and cold on our arrival – not a happy end to an otherwise enjoyable evening.

*

When I was employed by Kent County Council's Planning Department, I was lucky enough to attend two professional conferences, one year at Stirling University and another year at St. Andrew's University. The opening address at Stirling was given by Peter Walker, a Conservative minister. Walker had travelled to Scotland by overnight train. His address was timed at 10.00 a.m. He looked completely worn out. Nevertheless, he spoke fluently, with no notes, for half an hour or more. It was most impressive.

Before I move on from Scotland, I should mention several visits to that country made from cruise ships. One year *Swan Hellenic* commissioned the mail ship *St. Helena* for a cruise from Cardiff along the west coast of Britain, as far north as Skye. There was great excitement among the crew when the ship anchored at sea, not at the quayside, and passengers disembarked on the ship's lifeboats. Clearly the lifeboats had never before been put to such use. The standard ship run was to St. Helena and on to South Africa where, at both places, she could be berthed at the quayside. On our cruise, the officers and crew had great fun in getting passengers on board the lifeboats and then getting the boats to the quay. But all went well. There were no mishaps.

Subsequent cruises took me as far north as Shetland and the Orkney Islands and to Scotland's east coast. Once we put in to Invergordon and took a coach to Dunrobin Castle. Dunrobin was the ancient seat of the Sutherland earls, many of whose portraits still adorn the castle walls. We had an inexperienced guide taking us round the castle. She failed to tell us what we were about to see before we got there, or to collect us together before she spoke to us. I had to fill the gaps!

On another occasion we put in to Leith where we stayed overnight. I went to the Edinburgh Tattoo. Shortly after we took our seats, packed in like sardines, the heavens opened. It poured unmercifully and incessantly during the whole show. I returned to the ship like a drenched rat, immediately stripped and had a hot tub.

*

My penchant for visiting Scotland did not hinder visits to other parts of the British Isles. I have had three memorable trips to Eire: the first was a motoring trip with my mother. We spent a couple of nights in Dublin and then drove across Eire to the Ring of Kerry. The other two memorable trips to Eire were for the opera festivals at Wexford, already mentioned..

I have visited Wales several times: again, the first was a motoring trip with my mother. We stayed at Dolgellau. In those early days in my life, in order to save the high cost of hotel drinks, I used to travel with a bottle of gin in the car. I asked a local in Dolgellau where I could buy tonic water to add to my gin. She understood the word *tonic* and directed me to a chemist! The second time I went to Wales I was on my own. I stayed in Tenby and visited much of Pembrokeshire. Three times I have been to Cardiff for operatic holidays.

My visits to Northern Ireland have been restricted to day trips from cruise ships. Cruises have also taken me to Dublin and Cork in Eire.

I spent a few summer days in the Isle of Man as the guest of an old colleague from Northern Rhodesia who had retired there.

*

It will be recalled that Tommy, my father, was born in Calcutta. He was the fifth generation of Sutherlands to have lived in Calcutta. I was easily persuaded to visit India. This I did by flying to Calcutta and there boarding a cruise ship which circumnavigated India, ending up in Bombay (now Mumbai).

Calcutta was a city of faded glory. Many of the buildings built by the British when Calcutta was the seat of government were in need of maintenance. But far more distressing was the abject poverty of many Calcutta citizens. People were living on the pavements and washing in the gutters. Begging was rife. One of the lecturers on our ship was Sir David Goodall, a previous British High Commissioner in India. He said that India's population was increasing annually by an amount equivalent to the total population of Australia. India's agriculture and industry could not possibly give employment to such large numbers, he said.

In our journey round India, we diverted to stop at Galle in Sri Lanka (formerly Ceylon). Diana Murray (the widow of Jock Murray (the publisher) and I shared a taxi to visit the sites of Galle.

The Governor of Ceylon in 1811 was General Sir Robert Brownrigg (1759-1833). The General was the brother of my (probable) ancestor John Studholme Brownrigg (d.1787). General Brownrigg conquered Kandy in 1815 and annexed the kingdom to Ceylon.

When in Galle, some of us took a coach to the fascinating town of Kandy where we lunched and later visited the Temple of the Tooth. But Buddha's tooth was not on display that day.

I revisited Sri Lanka briefly during one of my round-the-world cruises. On that occasion, my ship called at Colombo.

Cochin was a port-of-call on my round-India cruise. I took a boat trip on *The Backs*. I chatted to the Indian skipper of the boat. He was the proud father of a clever son. He asked me for my home address. In due course I received a nice letter from him enclosing a photograph of his wife and son. I sent him a book and some money for his son. There was no reply. Did my gift ever reach its destination? Perhaps it did, with the reaction "quest accomplished"!

Bombay, like Calcutta, was the scene of great poverty. But, unlike Calcutta, it was bustling and, in many respects, thriving. There was a marked contrast between the poor of the city and the ultra-rich, with their wives bedecked in beautiful silks and jewels.

I flew back to London from Bombay. The very same day I flew to Cape Town.

*

My father was born in India: my mother and her nine siblings were born in South Africa. Two of her brothers, Bertie and Douglas McJannet lived out their lives in South Africa. Heather, my sister, married a South African (Hardy Brownstein). To me, South Africa has always been treasured as a second home.

Bertie had a son and grandsons who live in South Africa. Thus the McJannet surname flourishes in that country. Bertie's only daughter, RuthMary also lives in South Africa, married to a South African. I will come back to my Uncle Douglas and my cousin RuthMary in a while.

Heather and Hardy and their two young daughters left South Africa in the 1950s, largely because they disliked the racial policies of the Afrikaans government (*apartheid*). The family travelled to England on the *Pretoria Castle* at the same time as Jean (my mother) and me (see illustration 50). But Heather and Hardy retained a holiday cottage at Constantia, in the Cape. It was my destination after my round-India cruise. I had had a previous holiday there, joined after a day or two by Heather. (Hardy was a stay-at-home). Cape Town and the Cape Peninsula are arguably my favourite holiday destination. The scenery and climate of the Cape are unsurpassable. In addition to the two holidays in Heather's cottage at Constantia and to stop-overs in Cape Town on my way to and from Northern Rhodesia, I have had the good fortune to visit the Cape on at least three other occasions.

One such occasion was a short overnight stay in Cape Town during a round-the-world cruises. Another occasion was during a group package holiday starting in Cape Town and ending at Durban. First, we stayed in a hotel at Newlands which was our headquarters for several visits to wine farms in the Cape. We then flew to Durban and travelled by coach to a charming chalet hotel overlooking Isandlwana. Isandlwana was the scene of a devastating defeat of British forces by the Zulus during the Anglo-Zulu War of 1879. We visited the sites of other engagements during that war. Then we spent a day or two in Hluhluwe Game Reserve, before motoring back to Durban for our flight home. I had visited Hluhluwe several years previously when Heather and I were the guests of RuthMary and her husband Edward Gilfillan who were then living in northern Natal.

Once when holidaying in the Cape, Heather and I stayed in *The Cellars* Hotel in Constantia. After a week or more, we were joined by RuthMary and Edward Gilfillan. The four of us then drove across the Karoo (Edward driving) to the Gilfillan home which was then at Kenton-on-Sea in the Eastern Cape. We had two night stops between Constantia and Kenton-on-Sea.

After leaving Constantia, we first stopped at Worcester in order to visit the Hugo Naudé Art Centre. Naudé (1869-1941), as mentioned previously, is a distinguished South African artist. He was born in Worcester. He was a close friend (perhaps a boy-friend) of my uncle Douglas. At the Worcester Art Centre we found a fine pencil sketch of Douglas by Naudé (see illustration 17), and one or two photographs of Douglas with Naudé.

*

I have already mentioned some of the cruises which I have enjoyed over the years. My first cruise, in the 1970s, was with *Swan Hellenic* on their ship *Orpheus*. A travel agency run by two brothers with the surname *Swan* was asked to organise tours for people interested in the antiquities of Greece. *Swan Hellenic* came into being. The company's third ship was the *Orpheus*. She was small (4,145 gross tonnage) and basic. Nevertheless she provided an excellent service. Several first class lecturers versed in ancient history and archaeology were engaged.

The *Orpheus* was laid up in the winter months and operated in the eastern Mediterranean for the remainder of the year. On one occasion, I was joining the *Orpheus* at Piraeus for her first cruise of the summer season. We flew to Athens and took coaches to Piraeus. There was a hiccup! We were told that the *Orpheus* was not quite ready to take passengers on board and that we would be taken to a local restaurant for dinner. During the course of the meal, we were told that the *Orpheus* was now on sea trials and that we would have to spend the night on shore. First class hotel accommodation was arranged for us and the following morning we had a guided tour of the Acropolis. Later in the day we eventually boarded the *Orpheus*. There was a complimentary bottle of wine in our cabins. On our return to England, there was a cheque for £150 awaiting us, in compensation for the lost day at sea. Such was the first class service provided by *Swan Hellenic*.

*Swan Hellenic* expanded dramatically. It took over a much larger ship in 1996. It operated throughout the year and widened its geographical horizons. The ship was the *Minerva* (12,500 gross tonnage). There was an inevitable dumbing down on what was on offer to passengers, many of whom had wider tastes than archaeology and ancient history. *Minerva's* main disadvantage for me was the shortage of single-occupancy cabins. The few that were available were interior cabins which were very cramped.

*Swan Hellenic* expanded yet again in 2003. They took over an even larger ship – the *Minerva II* (30,277 gross tonnage). I had one cruise on *Minerva II*, which was notable in that there was a large group of American passengers who were Harvard alumni. The Americans remained aloof. They had their own tables in the dining saloon, their own on-board lecturer and their own coaches for day trips. I frowned!

The shipping company became overstretched. *Minerva II* was sold to *Princess Cruises*. Lord Sterling purchased the brand name *Swan Hellenic* and bought back the original *Minerva I*.

Lord Sterling was a former Chairman of P&O, the shipping company firmly established as a premier shipping line by Sir Thomas Sutherland (see previous chapter).

*

I switched my affections from *Swan Hellenic* to *Saga.* A big plus is that cruises with *Saga* nearly always start and end either at Dover or at Southampton. Generally, there is no flying and no hassle at airports. Moreover there is a chauffer-driven car to take one to the port of departure and finally bring one back home.

Twice I circumnavigated the world on the *Saga Rose.* Each cruise was of more than three months duration. Each time I travelled westwards. That had the advantage of extending many days at sea into 25 hour days, as we passed through different international time zones. To compensate, we lost a calendar day when we crossed the International Date Line. But that was no hardship. (If one travelled eastwards round the world, one would gain a calendar day at the International Date Line, but many days at sea would be of 23 hours duration, only).

My first round-the-world cruise took me down the east coast of South America, followed by visits to the Falkland Islands and to Antarctica. We were able to land in Antarctica at two different locations. Then after traversing the Pacific Ocean, we called in at several ports in New Zealand and in Australia. I was particularly pleased to meet some Sutherland cousins in Australia, for the first time. Two of my father's sisters had married Australians.

On my second round-the world cruise (in 2009) we sailed along the Panama Canal and took a southerly route along the west coast of South America. I left the ship at Lima, flew to Cuzco and visited Machu Pichu. After three days, I rejoined the ship at Callao. Another highlight of this particular cruise was a day on a private island in the Maldives. The *Saga Rose* dropped anchor and we were all ferried ashore to a small tropical island which had been set aside for our exclusive use for the day. On our island, the ship's chefs provided us with a magnificent barbecue lunch, the ship's band serenaded us and the champagne flowed.

It was an unforgettable experience.

I kept a record of the amount of food and drink consumed on the *Saga Rose,* during the 2009 cruise (of 33,344 nautical miles). We consumed 5,488 litres of ice cream, 147,660 kilograms of fresh fruit, 75,400 kilograms of fresh vegetables, 65,700 bottles of water, 10,600 bottles of wine and 22,470 cans of beer. Needless to say, the menus were invariably excellent.

The 2009 cruise was billed as a *Commonwealth Cruise*. We visited no less than 30 commonwealth countries.

During both world cruises the *Saga Rose* berthed in the heart of Sydney, with Sydney's famous opera house in full view. On each occasion I had a night at the opera.

*

I made friends with one of the on-board lecturers during a *Swan Hellenic* cruise in the Mediterranean. He had been the Dean of Christ Church, Oxford. The Reverend Dr Eric Heaton invited me to have a drink with him before dinner one evening. Rachel, his wife, was unable to join us: she was on duty in the ship's library. When Eric and I went in to dinner, he invited me to sit at the table he shared with other on-board lecturers and their wives. I asked Rachel whether she would prefer red or white wine. Eric immediately said "leave that to me". I demurred. "But **you** have just bought me a drink before dinner. It is **my** turn now". It transpired that the lecturers got all their drinks free. Eric ordered bottles of red, white and rosé wines!

We spent Easter Sunday at sea. Eric officiated at the 8 a.m. Holy Communion Service, helped by a passenger who was a parson. Far too much wine had been consecrated. After we had received our sip of wine, there were two half-full chalices which had to be emptied. Eric had no trouble in emptying one of them, but the parson who was helping struggled to empty the other one. He took a small sip and paused, another small sip and paused. Eric gently and deftly removed the chalice from his hands and swiftly quaffed what remained in it!

During this cruise we put in at Ashdod and went by coach to Jerusalem. I was amazed to see how well the land had been developed since 1948, the year I quit Palestine. The local guide on the coach was a young Jew who had migrated to Israel from the United States. He found it impossible to say the word *Palestine*. He spoke only of the West Bank and the Gaza Strip.

En route to Jerusalem we stopped on the shore of the Sea of Galilee and went for a sail on that Sea. The majority of the passengers on the boat were not from our cruise ship. Notwithstanding, Eric Heaton asked the skipper to silence the engines. He then recited *The Beatitudes*. It was most moving.

When I left Jerusalem in 1948, it was predominantly an Arab city, with Jewish and Christian minorities. Israel set about correcting that. It established *Greater Jerusalem* by incorporating large areas of land surrounding the city where it built satellite settlements populated by Jews. Jews became the majority population in Greater Jerusalem.

The Old City of Jerusalem was out of bounds when I was stationed in Palestine. It was a great experience to enter the Old City for the first time and to visit the Muslim Dome of the Rock and the Wailing Wall. Racial tension between the Arab and Jew residents was palpable. Israeli troops were in evidence everywhere.

*

Eric Heaton was a first class lecturer. Other outstanding lecturers on my cruises whom I can recall include a group of 4 lecturers from the *Scott Polar Research Institute* in Cambridge who joined the *Saga Rose* when she was in the Antarctic. Not only were their talks illuminating: one evening they read extracts from the diaries of Scott and his fellow explorers. This lasted for about an hour and replaced the customary late night entertainment on board. No applause was allowed. Many a tear was shed.

The BBC journalist John Cole was another interesting lecturer. I have already mentioned his anecdote about Winston Churchill.

It was always refreshing to have a humorous on-board lecturer. One such was an Indian who was a National Health Doctor of Medicine. Two of his talks were about the vagaries of the English language. He said "one expects to **run** on one's feet and **smell** with one's nose. But, oh no! The English have it that your **nose** runs and your **feet** smell"! I gave him another anomaly for his collection. An unruly child is told "sit **down**" and as soon as it has done so, it is told "sit **up**".

Another humorist was the cartoonist Gerald Scarfe. He was asked if he had drawn any cartoons of passengers. "No", he replied, "but I have made some drawings of hippos"!

It has to be said that some lecturers were disappointing. The Right Rev. Richard Harries, renowned for his talks on the radio called *Thought for the Day*, simply read from the papers he held in his hand. Moreover, he occasionally failed to decipher his own handwriting and read out the wrong word. He gave the impression that he had come simply to enjoy himself on the cruise – not to give lectures.

The same criticism could be made of Sir John Keegan, the eminent military historian. His talks were ill prepared and poorly delivered. The cruise was in the Black Sea with its pronounced military history. One of John's talks was given on the site of the battle of Balaclava during the Crimean War. I happened to know the part played by the *Sutherland Highlanders* during the battle (*The Thin Red Line*). John had a different version. I whispered to the retired Colonel standing beside me "Keegan is wrong". "Quite so, my boy", he said. "Speak up"! But I hadn't the courage to "speak up" in front of 100 or more fellow passengers. However, when I got home I wrote to John and asked him to give me his source. To his great credit he replied "I am mortified. You are quite right: I was quite wrong".

In the following year, John gave the London Library annual lecture at the Royal Geographical Society headquarters. His subject was First and Second World War authors. It was a brilliant lecture. The London literati were not to be treated so cavalierly as a bunch of passengers on a cruise ship!

## Chapter 15

# RUSSIA

Before I took up cruising as a pastime, I had a two week package holiday in Russia. The year was 1987. Russia was still a communist super-power. Gorbachev was the Russian President.

I travelled by air to Leningrad (now St. Petersburg), had a week there, took an overnight train to Moscow, had another week there and then flew home. The travel agent was *Serenissima,* which was then in the ownership of John Julius Norwich. His daughter, Artemis Cooper was the assistant tour leader in Leningrad. The whole tour was led, admirably led, by Prince George Galitzine. Despite George's noble descent, he was as British as they come. He had been an officer in the Welsh Guards, but he still spoke Russian fluently. I was concerned that the locals might be offended by the presence of a White Russian Prince. In fact, they showed him great respect.

Artemis Cooper, George Galitzune's assistant in Leningrad, is now the wife of the eminent military historian Antony Beevor. She, herself, is a published author. I met them both at a piano recital in Ewelme church, when I was staying with my friends Robert and Joan Clive, several years later.

*

The Russians foisted an Intourist "guide" on us: one in Leningrad, another in Moscow. Both were women. Their overriding duty seemed to be to ensure that we always stayed in our group, and never strayed. I will give two examples. Two fellow travellers and I wished to go to the Mariinsky Theatre in Leningrad one evening to see the ballet. I asked the hotel receptionist if she could get tickets for us. "How many of your group wish to go" she enquired? "I have no idea" I said. "Then ask your Intourist guide to find out" was the response. Several of us decided to go to the ballet. Tickets were secured, official transport was laid on and we were accompanied by a Russian official.

On another occasion, one or two of us wanted to use the toilets in the grounds of a palace in Leningrad. The stench from the public toilets carried far and wide. Two men in our group therefore decided to find a friendly tree, in order to relieve themselves. "Stay in group" was the immediate injunction from the Intourist guide. Notwithstanding, they wandered off – closely followed by the guide. She was concerned that they would escape her clutches. When she caught up with them, they were already relieving themselves. My young American friend, Robert Del Gatto said "and do ours look the same as they do in Russia"? His companion at the time laughed so much that he piddled on his shoes!

I felt that I was being singled out for strict observation when I was in Russia. Was it because a previous British ambassador to Russia shared a surname with me? But I was not related to Sir Iain Sutherland. Close scrutiny started when I arrived at Leningrad airport. The immigration official took ages before stamping my passport, talking the while to his colleagues and checking official-looking documents. In the *Astoria Hotel* where we all stayed, I would get strange telephone calls during the hours of darkness, presumably to check whether I was indeed in my bedroom.

When I finally flew home from Moscow airport, the customs official took an age in clearing my luggage. We had been warned by George Galitzine to declare any gold that we had on our entry documents and again on our departure documents. I duly declared a signet ring and a pair of cuff links. The customs official at Moscow airport (who had good English) said "open up your suitcase, please". He then proceeded slowly to unpack its contents. "Is there anything in particular you would like to see" I enquired? No response! In the bottom of the suitcase he pounced on my stud box, opened it and said "these cuff links are of gold". "Yes", I replied "and if you look at my papers you will see that I declared them on entry into Russia and again now". He duly checked my papers and found them in order. Whether or not this riled him, his next step was to take up my address book, and slowly turn over each page, ostensibly scrutinising them. Eventually he told me to repack my belongings. The overall delay was so extensive that I and my fellow travellers thought I might miss our scheduled flight home. One dared not remonstrate.

Here are two or three examples of how hidebound the Russians were under communist rule. The receptionist at the *Astoria Hotel* told me that we were the last group to stay there, before the hotel was completely remodernised. "Then why", I asked "is the corridor in the basement currently being redecorated"? "Because that is in the 5-year plan" was her serious reply!

I asked the *Astoria Hotel* receptionist to cash a sterling traveller's cheque into sterling, one of the currencies accepted by the shops open exclusively to tourists. The receptionist refused my request. I then asked for directions to the nearest bank. "There is no bank in Leningrad which will cash a sterling traveller's cheque" came the curt reply. "So how do I get some more money" I asked? "You will have to buy something in a tourist shop with a traveller's cheque and ask for the change in sterling".

Gorbachev had decreed that no alcohol could be purchased before 2 p.m. As a result, lunch in the hotel was never served before that hour. If one happened to be out at, say 1 p.m., one saw large queues outside the liquour shops, waiting for them to open. It is doubtful whether Gorbachev's decree had any effect on alcohol consumption by the Russians – and it was an irritant to citizens and tourists alike.

Although it was mid-October when I was in Moscow, the weather was still warm. Nonetheless, the radiator in my hotel bedroom was on full blast. I could find no way of turning it off, or of lowering the setting. When the management was asked to sort this out, the reply came that winter was deemed to start on October 1st. The radiators were then switched on throughout the hotel and would remain on until next spring. In no way could one radiator be shut down or adjusted.

While in Moscow, we travelled north to Yaroslavl and

went on a short river trip on the Volga. The young man in charge of the boat was most courteous and spoke good English. “Please, please” he said “don’t take any photographs of bridges or buildings on the river banks. I will lose my job if it is found that you have taken any such photographs”. We complied, of course, but no bridge or building was worth a second glance. None appeared to have any strategic significance.

*

Despite Gorbachev’s policy of *glasnost*, life for the Russians in the 1980s was still repressive, authoritarian and doctrinaire.

When we were having lunch in a restaurant outside Moscow, I noticed that the ever-present Intourist guide was sitting at a table on her own. I decided to join her. She had excellent English and was intelligent. During our conversation, we talked about Hitler’s invasion of Russia and Leningrad’s miraculous survival. (Hitler was going to announce the fall of Leningrad from the balcony of the *Astoria Hotel* where we had been staying. A menu for the subsequent banquet had already been prepared). The Intourist guide was adamant that Russia had won the war against Nazi Germany, and that Britain and the United States only entered the war after it was clear that Russia had won it. Nothing I said could persuade her otherwise. I asked her for her opinion of Stalin. She said that the Stalin era was now under review. Meanwhile she could not commit herself to any definite opinion. I also asked her how it was that she spoke such good English. “I read as much in English as I can” she said. “But there are no English books or papers to be had” I replied. She then said she relied on gifts from tourists, such as me. I duly gave her a copy of Adam Smith’s *Wealth of Nations*. I wonder if she read it and, if so, what she made of it!

We went to a ballet performance in the Bolshoi Theatre in Moscow. The man driving the coach which took us from our hotel to the theatre told us that he had trained to become an operatic singer, but he had finally failed to make the grade. He was then **directed** to be a coach driver. How authoritarian! How insensitive! It so happened that we had a spare ticket to the ballet because Shirley Anglesey (the Marchioness of Anglesey), one of our number, had a prior official engagement that evening. We invited our coach driver to take over her ticket. He was delighted, of course, if only to enter the hallowed hall where so many of his operatic idols had sung. We were rewarded. On the way back to our hotel, the coach driver deviated from the direct route and sang one operatic aria after another as he ambled along Moscow's back streets. He had a delightful baritone voice. His kindness added greatly to the pleasure of our evening.

*

The hotel in Moscow where we were staying overlooked Red Square. I was looking at the traffic in the Square one evening, from my bedroom window. It was warm, but it was pouring with rain. Policemen, well protected from the elements, repeatedly stopped individual cars and demanded to see the papers of the driver. In some instances a driver was required to get out of his vehicle and stand and answer questions, in shirtsleeves, in the heavy rain. It was inhuman.

I asked our ever-present Intourist guide at breakfast next morning why the police had been behaving that way. She said that the drivers had probably committed a traffic offence. "Certainly none that I could see", I said. "Perhaps", she replied, "at an earlier junction". That excuse seemed most unlikely to me. Whether or not there was a valid reason for the police behaviour, one was left with the feeling that they were cruelly showing just who was boss.

We were warned that the Moscow police were zealous in monitoring the behaviour of pedestrians. "Never attempt to cross a road, other than at a designated pedestrian crossing when the crossing light is in your favour". I temporarily forgot this injunction. I was taking photographs in the Kremlin when I stepped off the pavement into the carriageway – only a pace – in order to get a better angle for the picture I was after. There was no quiet, civil admonition. Immediately police whistles were blown and police truncheons were raised. I felt like a criminal.

Perhaps it is because the communist state took away

so much power and discretion from the individual citizen that, when a policeman or other official was given certain powers, those powers were exercised indiscriminately and excessively. It compensated!

*

Although it was nearly thirty years since the end of hostilities, living conditions in Russia were still austere. As tourists, we had been advised to take with us soap, toilet paper and a bath plug. This proved to be sensible advice. Even in some of the best hotels, plumbing and sewerage left a lot to be desired.

At a night out at the ballet, few Russians were smartly dressed – and it was evident that there was a lack of soap for personal hygiene.

Such luxury goods that were available could be purchased only with dollars, pounds sterling or deutschmarks, in foreign-currency shops (*Beriozka)*. This put them out of the reach of most citizens. When I was in Moscow, I noticed a long queue outside *Gum*, the renowned departmental store in Red Square. The reason for the queue was that *Gum* had just received a consignment of chocolate cakes. Clearly, chocolate cakes were not readily available on a daily basis.

The menus in hotels and restaurants were basic. One was never offered exotic fruit, for example; only windfall apples. Caviar and vodka, on the other hand, seemed to be plentiful and reasonably priced.

No doubt housing, health care and education were heavily subsidised by the state. That was certainly so in the case of public transport, in my experience. George Galitzine took me on a tram ride in Leningrad from one end of the city to the other in order to see the graves of some of Russia's classical musicians (Glinka, Mussorgsky, Rimsky-Korsakov, and Tchaikovsky) in the Tikhvin Cemetery. The tram ride cost practically nothing. Then in Moscow, George Galitzine and I travelled on the metro with a very cheap rover ticket. This enabled us to stop and admire the impressive architectural features at numerous underground stations.

The train journey from Leningrad to Moscow was also inexpensive. I shared a sleeping car with George Galitzine. George said that when the railway was being built, the construction company had difficulties in acquiring some of the necessary land on the route. They went to see the Tsar. The Tsar asked for a map and a straight edge. He then drew a straight line between the two cities and said "build the railway on this line. If you have any trouble with the landowners on this route, refer them to me". There was no trouble with landowners, but the straight line route failed to connect with some intermediary major settlements.

There was an amusing incident when George took us on one of our visits to The Hermitage in Leningrad. He asked a curator to open the rooms which housed a collection of French furniture. He was told that it was temporarily closed. George then said "Look! I am escorting a group from England who are furniture connoisseurs and who especially want to see your wonderful collection of French furniture". After some huffing and puffing, keys were produced and the rooms were unlocked. We walked straight past the furniture to a window overlooking Palace Square. George drew back a corner of the curtain. There, inscribed in English with a diamond on the glass window-pane, was "I watched the parade here on . . . . Nicholas". The so-called furniture connoisseurs then left that part of the museum!

The Hermitage, of course, deserves many visits and its magnificent collection deserves much study. I have been fortunate in making return visits on two occasions, in the course of Baltic cruises. On the second occasion, the Hermitage was closed to the general public in the evening. After an hour looking at some of the art masterpieces in relative quiet, a group from our ship was entertained to an orchestral concert given in one of the salons, followed by a glass of champagne.

Another amusing incident happened when a group of us from Moscow spent a night in an old monastery which had been converted into tourist accommodation. There was a party of Swedes also staying there at the time. A Swedish lady took a great fancy to John Guest, who was in our group. She besought

John to tell her the number of his chalet, where he would be passing the night. John declined. He asked me to knock on the partition between his bedroom and my adjoining bedroom at a specified time next morning, so as to arouse him. Before that specified time, I heard a banging on John's bedroom door. I later asked him who had woken him. "It was that wretched Swedish woman", he said. "Somehow or other, she found out the number of our chalet. I thought it was you knocking so I got up, clad only in my pyjamas, and opened the door. I hastily slammed it shut in her face". The incident was reported to the Swede courier looking after the Swedish tourists. She apologised and said that the woman had been a confounded pest on many occasions during their tour.

John Guest was a well-known figure in the world of publishing. He was a close friend of Shirley Anglesey whose father was the novelist and dramatist Charles Morgan. Shirley, it will be remembered, was one of the participants in *Serenissima's* Moscow party. A few years after the Moscow trip, I went to a National Trust lecture in the Purcell Room (on the South Bank) which was given by Shirley Anglesey's husband. The lecture was principally about *Plas Newydd*, the ancestral home of the Angleseys, but now in the ownership of the National Trust. *Plas Newydd* is famous for its association with the artist Rex Whistler. I did not know that at the time.

I was not surprised to find John Guest waiting, like me, to enter the Purcell Room for the National Trust Lecture. John told me, with some pride that he owned a Whistler. In my ignorance, I thought he was referring to the rather more prestigious artist J.M. Whistler!

Shirley Anglesey invited John and me to go behind the scenes and speak to the Marquess, after his lecture. Sadly, I had to decline. I had a train to catch to get me home to Maidstone.

*

One makes close friends and passing acquaintances on a protracted tour such as was my first visit to Russia. Two close friends from the Leningrad week were Bettie Knott who lived in St John's Wood, London, and Robert Del Gatto, an American banker then living in New York. I have already mentioned Robert. We keep in touch and whenever he visits England we meet up. After Russia, Bettie and I had numerous outings together in London, principally for visits to the opera or to the ballet. Bettie was a keen admirer of Russian arts. When she died, she left me two items of antique furniture.

A year or two after my Russian adventure, George Galitzine gave an illustrated talk at the British Museum about St. Petersburg (as Leningrad had by then become, once again). Bettie Knott, Elspeth Veale (another friend from the Leningrad days) and I went to George's talk. It was excellent, with some wonderful photographs. At the end, I approached George, congratulated him and said "I don't know how many of your women admirers in the audience have spent or would like to spend a night with you, but I guess I am the only male member of the audience who has spent a night with you"! George remembered, of course, our overnight train journey from Leningrad to Moscow.

A close friend from the Moscow week was Dora Wirth. Dora was a remarkable woman: a Jew born in Russia who had to flee to Danzig (Gdansk) as a young child with her parents. Soon she was fluent in her native tongue and in Polish, German and English. She married a German. They lived in London. Two sons were born. Dora worked for the Beaverbrook press translating Hitler's 1930 speeches into English. Her husband died and Dora was faced with the daunting task of bringing up two teenage sons on her own in her newly adopted country. She realised that her one skill was foreign languages. She set about establishing a translation business, specialising in the translation of medical pamphlets and tracts written by pharmaceutical companies. The business flourished. One son, after he had grown up, joined the business. Dora owned a house and business premises in central London and a flat in Brighton. She was always very kind to me and often entertained me both in London and in Brighton.

*

There were two American men in the Moscow contingent who

were opera enthusiasts. They said that they were Friends of Glyndebourne and visited Glyndebourne every year. I told them how lucky they were. I lived fairly close to Glyndebourne, but very seldom could I get a ticket to an opera there. I couldn't become a Friend: there was a long waiting list. Bob Goodman, one of the Americans, kept in touch with me. As a Friend of Glyndebourne, he was able to get two tickets to each opera, whereas he needed only one. Likewise his companion could get two tickets, but needed only one. Out of the goodness of their hearts they invited me to join them for an opera at Glyndebourne in two successive years.

Chapter 16

# GARDENING

I am no expert gardener, but for many years I was a member of the Royal Horticultural Society (RHS) and I have a passion for flowers. When I worked in London, I regularly attended the RHS shows at St. Vincent's Square, and I have been a frequent visitor to the Chelsea Flower Show. I have also been a Friend of the Royal Botanic Gardens, Kew.

Gardening in Northern Rhodesia was not easy. The really well-kept gardens belonged to people who could afford to pay for a lot of water. Water in the major towns was always available, but at a cost. In Choma, where there was no piped water supply, I collected all the bath water in a large drum sunk in the ground outside my bathroom and used that to water my garden.

When I lived in Lusaka, my pride and joy was a white lantana hedge. When it was in full bloom, the hedge appeared as if it was covered with a blanket of snow. Alas, the Government decreed that lantana was a noxious weed. There were impenetrable acres of the common, cherry-pie variety in certain areas. No cognizance was given to the fact that the white variety was a relative rarity. I had never seen it elsewhere. Certainly, it was not choking up vast areas of land. When I returned from my final overseas leave, I found that my glorious white lantana hedge had been grubbed up by the Public Works Department.

South Africa which I have frequently visited has a world famous flora. I have never visited Namaqualand, but I have seen the Kirstenbosch Botanical Gardens in Cape Town at different times of the year. As well as the Cape flora, I have seen a magnificent display of wild flowers in the Drakensberg Mountains. For many years I had a small collection of books on South African flora.

*

When I lived in Maidstone, Kent, I had only a small garden. It was bounded on the north and west by an old brick wall (part of the original *Foley Park Estate*) which was ideal for climbers. The southern boundary abutted the pavement and had to be kept free of hedges or walls exceeding four feet in height. This had its drawbacks. There was no privacy. The garden could be invaded by neighbouring cats and dogs, and by children retrieving their balls. Nevertheless, I managed to create an attractive garden, which was often admired by passing pedestrians.

Kent is popularly known as the *Garden of England.* That is because, historically, it had many small **hop** gardens. Today, most of the hop gardens have disappeared, but Kent can boast some magnificent **flower** gardens. Perhaps the best known flower garden in Kent is Sissinghurst. It was created by Vita Sackville West and her husband Harold Nicolson. It is now owned by the National Trust. Sissinghurst Castle and garden attract thousands of visitors every year. I was a frequent visitor when I lived in Kent. Nigel Nicolson, Harold and Vita's son used to live in a wing of the castle. In an after-luncheon speech to the Kent Garden Trust, Nigel said that visitors to Sissinghurst sometimes asked him the name of an unusual plant, for which the name plate had gone. Nigel was not a plantsman, so he would invent a name. The visitor carefully recorded this spurious name in his or her notebook. A few weeks later, Nigel would get a letter saying "I have been in touch with several specialist nurseries. None of them knows this plant. Do you think you could please send me a cutting, or some seeds"?

Just over the Kent boundary, in Sussex, is another world famous garden. Great Dixter was created by Christopher Lloyd. I was a frequent visitor. Christopher Lloyd could often be seen working in his garden, but he did not like to engage in conversation with visitors. He was as adept with his pen as he was with his planting. He wrote many interesting books and was a regular contributor to *Country Life.*

I became a member of the Kent Garden Trust and served on their events committee. Usually we arranged visits to privately owned gardens in Kent. Once I organised a trip to Hampton Court.

When I was preparing to move from Maidstone to Aldeburgh, I wondered how I might dispose of my (by then) considerable collection of gardening books. Included in the collection was a full set of the re-issued *Curteiss' Botanical Magazine*. I consulted the RHS about the disposal of the latter. Their only suggestion was to place an advertisement in their magazine *Garden* – at considerable expense. Indeed, the cost of a small advertisement might well have exceeded the sale value of the magazines! I then consulted the Royal Botanical Garden, Kew. Kew put me in touch with a second-hand book dealer, who had previously worked at Kew. He agreed to purchase my set of magazines, at a very fair price. I asked him if he would be interested in further purchases. The answer was "yes". He went through my catalogue of gardening books and made numerous (also very reasonable) offers, which I gladly accepted. My niece, Rosemary, herself a keen gardener, then had her pick of the remaining books. She took about 20, most of them relating to South African flora. (Rosemary was born in South Africa). The rest of my collection of gardening books was boxed up and donated to the Kent Garden Trust, for sale at their meetings.

*

The very first package holiday I took was a visit to Corsica. It was billed as a *gardens tour*, but in fact there are few floriferous gardens in that beautiful island – neither in public nor in private ownership. The one or two gardens which we did visit were pretty ordinary, by English standards. The indigenous vegetation, however, was attractive. Robert and Joan Clive were also on this tour. We became great friends. We discovered that Joan's birthday and mine were only a day apart. In subsequent years, Joan would invite me to join her for a joint celebration of our birthdays. She lived in Ewelme, Oxfordshire, where she had created a fabulous garden which she opened to the public.

One year, shortly after Robert's death, Joan and I celebrated our birthdays by lunching at Cliveden – then a luxury country house hotel and formerly the scene of the notorious John Profumo/Christine Keeler affair. After lunch Joan and I were invited to take a look at the guest bedroom suites. It was a revelation to find that there was a card on the door of each suite giving the names of the occupants the following night. In more than one instance the card bore the name of a titled man and of an unrelated woman!

I visited Holland during tulip time in the spring of 1989, on a trip organised by *Swan Hellenic*. Our "home" was a river boat – the M.V. *Victoria Regia.* In the bulb fields and public gardens there were acres upon acres of tulips in serried rows, all in seemingly perfect condition, but of little appeal to a gardener. Of particular interest, however, were the auction houses – vast covered areas in which vans and lorries bustled to and fro. The flowers for sale were paraded around one of several auction floors, in clear view of serried rows of bidders. A big clock displayed a price. The hand of the clock started to rotate, the price gradually falling. A bidder pressed a button, the clock immediately stopped, a bargain had been struck at the price indicated on the clock and the purchased flowers were immediately whisked off and were on their way to their final destination – perhaps by air to Paris or London. It was all wonderfully efficient.

After dinner on board the *Victoria Regia* on a Saturday evening, I ventured into Amsterdam. My friend (and cousin?) Henry Brownrigg had told me that Amsterdam was his favourite European city. I have to say I was sorely disappointed. The city was *en fête* – possibly in celebration of the Dutch Queen's birthday. Whatever the reason, the centre was thronged with drunken revellers. There was vomiting on the pavements. The roads were ankle deep in discarded bottles, beer cans and food wrappings. Men were openly urinating in shop doorways. On my return to the ship, I walked down a road where prostitutes were disporting themselves, in various stages of undress, in gaudily lit windows, trying to solicit trade. Only during the day, when we took to canal boats and saw something of Amsterdam from its waterways, was my disgust for the city slightly assuaged. In many ways, the city is the Venice of the north. It was the city's inhabitants and, no doubt, its many visitors that had repelled me.

I have visited Amsterdam in later years and have been more favourably impressed. A highlight on one of these occasions was a visit to the Anne Frank (1929-1945) Museum.

*

In July 1992, Heather and I joined a small party on a garden tour in Shropshire. We stayed in the renowned *Feathers Hotel* in Ludlow. We got in touch with an Australian first cousin who was then living in Clun. Jean (Armstrong) was a niece of Tommy. We had never met before.

It was an ideal time of the year to be visiting gardens. They were in their full flush of summer splendour. We saw several private gardens, of different types, but none, in my view, surpassed Sissinghurst or Great Dixter in beauty.

Our tour ended in tragedy. I returned to Maidstone, leaving Heather in her London flat. She rang Hardy (her husband) and said that she would return to their home in Yorkshire (which also had a beautiful garden) on the following day. Since it would be a Sunday, when train services can be erratic, Heather told Hardy not to meet her at York station. She would take a taxi out to their village (Howsham). It was a hot July afternoon. The lawns had just been mown. Hardy was lying down peacefully on one of the mown lawns. He was not asleep. He had had a massive heart attack and had died.

*

One year, Heather and I went on a gardening excursion to the Italian Lake District. As well as visiting numerous outstanding gardens, we spent a day at the Thyssen gallery. Our excellent tour leader was J.B. (John) Paton. His wife Mary was also travelling with us. John and Mary became our great friends. They live not far from Aldeburgh, and were most kind to both Heather and me when we came to live in Suffolk. John had been the horticultural adviser to the Commonwealth War Graves Commission. He is a judge at the Chelsea Flower Show. One could not have found a better tour leader.

*Anitra*, for that was the nickname I gave her, was one of our party. She was attractive, sparkling, intelligent and a lot younger than the rest of us. She was always pleased to join Heather and me. We got to know her quite well, but thought there was a sorrow somewhere in her life, about which she didn't wish to speak. I saw a lot of Anitra after our return to England.

At the Festival Hall in London, Anitra and I were dining in the restaurant, before a concert. She was bubbling over with excitement. She told me all. When she was very young and looking after her ailing mother, an older, married man took advantage of her naivety, with the inevitable result that she had a son by him. The man refused to break up his marriage and marry Anitra. So, with considerable heartbreak, Anitra had the baby adopted. By the time of our meeting at the Festival Hall, this son was in his late teens. Anitra had heard that very day, from the adoption agency, that her son wanted to get in touch with her. The agency would pave the way for a meeting, if she so wished. Anitra hadn't dared tell Heather and me about this incident. She feared that we might turn our backs on her. I assured Anitra that she would always be our good friend. What she had now told me made absolutely no difference to that.

I hoped the reunion between mother and son would bring Anitra great happiness. I am sorry to record that it caused her further distress. Anitra has written all about it in a published book.

Some time later, a divorced man with a physical disability proposed to Anitra. She asked me if I thought it would be a successful marriage. I expressed some doubts. If there was love on both sides, so be it. But it seemed to me that Anitra wasn't truly in love with him. I feared, as she did, that this man's interest in Anitra was as his secretary and nurse. No marriage ensued.

Anitra had been William Lyne's secretary at the Wigmore Hall. Lyne gave her two complimentary tickets for the opening recital of the 1990 season. Margaret Price was to be the soloist. Anitra invited me to join her. Before the recital began, Lyne invited us backstage for a glass of champagne after the concert was over. Backstage, there was a throng of people, none of whom I knew or even recognized. In a while, Margaret Price and her husband left. I asked one of the staff whether the room in which we were having our drinks was, in fact, the artists' dressing room. It seemed to me to be far too large for that. "No", he said. He showed me where the artists' dressing room was. "Go in and have a look round. No one is there now". In went Anitra and I. The room was full of bouquets which had been presented to Margaret Price and left behind. Round the walls were signed photographs of many artists who had performed in the Wigmore Hall, over the years. Anitra noticed that one photograph had been turned to face the wall. She asked me to look and see whose photograph it was. It was Jessye Norman's! Margaret Price didn't want another top soprano looking down on her, before her recital!

I have kept in touch with Anitra, but this has rather degenerated into an exchange of news and greetings at Christmas. However, I was having a drink in the bar at the Wigmore Hall, one evening, when an attractive woman threw her arms around me and gave me a big hug. She noted my surprise and said "you don't recognize me, do you"? The hair style was different and there was a degree of maturity, but I was delighted to find that it was dear Anitra – still as sparkling as ever. I am happy to record that soon after this unexpected meeting Anitra entered into a very happy marriage.

Anitra's story has taken me away from gardening and back to music. But, after all, these have been two of my abiding interests.

*

There is another gardening holiday worthy of note. In the spring of 2006, Heather and I went on a short cruise which had a garden theme. We sailed from Harwich to the Channel Islands and back on the *Van Gogh.* We were accommodated in a suite comprising a large bedroom, a large sitting room (which we converted into a second bedroom) and a fully equipped bathroom. Apart from this accommodation, the *Van Gogh* had little to recommend it. But some of the garden visits were first class, including Monet's garden at Givenchy, Tresco Abbey Gardens and the Eden Project near Falmouth.

*

In Aldeburgh I have a small patio garden, as does Heather, who is my neighbour. We have removed the dividing fence between us and created a much larger garden as a result. The soil is quite different from that at Maidstone, but I have managed to establish a relatively attractive garden. The only snag is that, with advancing years, the flower beds seem to get lower and lower!

*

*A garden is a lovesome thing, God wot.*
*The Glory of the Garden it abideth not in words!*

72. Garden at 20 Saxons Drive, Maidstone

73. Garden at 20 Saxons Drive, Maidstone

74. Garden at 20 Saxons Drive, Maidstone

75. Author with Joan Clive at Sissinghurst

Chapter 17

# MORE LEISURE PURSUITS

Human relationships and a career or occupation are, perhaps, the most important elements in the lives of most people. Nevertheless, a surprising amount of one's time is devoted to other pursuits; perhaps for me more than for many others.

I have remained a bachelor throughout my life. Naturally, therefore, less of my time than that of a married man with a family has been devoted to human relationships. There was a mother, but no wife or children to care for.. As regards my career – or careers, as it turned out – there was always a deep commitment in time and energy, but much frustration.

When I took early retirement from my final career as a land use planner, it gave me more time and scope for recreation. In earlier chapters, I have described, in some detail, my interests in music, writing, travelling and gardening. But my recreations have extended further.

Genealogy has been a time-consuming interest. Like many people, I was interested to find out about my roots. The results of my genealogical researches in that regard are summarised in the first three chapters of this book. Genealogy also played a part in work on my book *A Fighting Clan* and on its unpublished sequel *And On They Fought*. My role as Clan Sutherland Society historian for five years also involved genealogical research from time to time.

As a result, I amassed a considerable collection of papers relating to members of my Clan (Sutherland). These papers have been donated to the Highland Archive at Inverness, catalogued under reference number HCA/D1316.

My mother's maiden surname of McJannet is relatively rare. I therefore decided to undertake a comprehensive McJannet (sometimes spelt McJannett) name search. The major result was an unpublished booklet of more than 100 pages which I entitled *Two McJannet Family Trees*. Each family was headed by a William McJannet. I came to the conclusion that the elder William McJannet (1699-1784) was a great uncle of the younger William McJannet (1759-1782), my forebear. I have donated my McJannet papers to the Scottish Genealogical Society in Edinburgh.

*

I have always been an avid reader – particularly of biographies. I got into the habit when I lived in Africa of giving away many books at the end of each tour, if I felt that they were inessential reference books or other books which I was unlikely to read a second time. When I moved from Maidstone to Aldeburgh, therefore, it was no real hardship to sell off (for little recompense) some twenty packing cases of books, in addition to the disposal of my gardening books, mentioned previously. Later, I donated all my books on military history to the Army & Navy Club, of which I am a member.

I also donated all my books on India to the British Association of Cemeteries in South Asia (BACSA), of which I am a member. BACSA has sold on many of these donated books to other members of the Association, thereby raising considerable funds which are put to good use towards the recording and maintenance of cemeteries of the many Europeans who died in India and elsewhere in South Asia. Several of my own ancestors were buried in India.

Now I continue to pass on many books to local charity shops, but my living room and my study still seem to be overflowing with books.

In former years in Africa, I used to review books for the local radio station. In Africa one turned one's hand to all sorts of things!

*

Outdoor pursuits have included photography, bird-watching and walking – none indulged in today!

I seldom photographed people: my photographs were

invariably of scenery, buildings or gardens. Too late, I came to realize that it is important to keep a record of what one's friends looked like. Such photographs have a wider than personal interest, whereas the photographs which I took could be boring to other people. I disposed of all of them when I packed up in Maidstone. I also got rid of my camera.

Kent was an ideal place for bird-watching, especially in the Medway estuary. I had a young friend, Antony Lucas, (illustration 76) who was a keen and knowledgeable ornithologist. We had many bird-watching expeditions together. In Suffolk there is the renowned bird sanctuary at Minsmere, which I visited several times when I was a member of the Royal Society for the Protection of Birds. I have also visited Slimbridge and several other bird sanctuaries both in England and in Africa.

Walking was a necessary part of my life in Africa as a land surveyor. But in England it became a favourite pastime. Wherever I have been, I have equipped myself with a footpath map. I have tried to see the local area, whether village or countryside, on foot. It is far more interesting than looking at it from a car window! (In any event, I am nearly always the driver, so my eye necessarily is on the road, not on the surrounding countryside). In Kent, over the years, I walked the length of the North Downs Way, from the Surrey border to Dover, section by section.

Cryptic crosswords have been a life-long pursuit: *The Times* every day until *The Times* became a tabloid newspaper, and then the *Daily Telegraph* each day. For many years I also completed the cryptic crosswords in *Country Life* and in the *Spectator*. I have won an occasional prize.

*

Much of my recreational time has been spent in playing bridge. I started playing bridge when I was a schoolboy. I played a bit when I was in the army, but it was not until the 1960s, when I was living in Lusaka that I took up the game in a big way. Lusaka had a thriving duplicate bridge club which held meetings once a week. My playing partner was Barbara Copeland, Dudley

Copeland's wife. Inclined to be a little nervous at first, Barbara developed into a first class player.

Duplicate bridge was organised by my great friend P.P. (Peter) Walker. Peter and his first wife, Anna were also great friends of my mother, Jean. Peter became my partner in duplicate bridge matches against Southern Rhodesia and the Belgian Congo. We also played for Northern Rhodesia in a team of four, with a surgeon and a plumber – both good players (illustration 78). As well as matches in Lusaka, there were matches in Salisbury (Harare) and on the Copperbelt. It is fair, if rather immodest, to say that we always acquitted ourselves well.

There was plenty of domestic (rubber) bridge in Lusaka, as well as club bridge. Peter and my surgeon friend, J.J. (Jimmy) Macpherson were regular participants in a men's four. We were usually joined by J.G. (John) Doubleday, or sometimes by the Registrar or Assistant Registrar of Deeds (both Irish solicitors). John Doubleday and his girlfriend (later his wife) Ruth Buchan, and John and Enid Turner often participated in mixed gender family bridge. All in all, I probably played bridge on an average of three evenings each week. Stakes were relatively low; standards were relatively high. One of the ladies I occasionally played rubber bridge with was called Liz Smelt. She told me her brother, Tony, had the initials **A.W.C.S**(melt)! What insensitive parents!

Lasting friendships were made at the bridge table. In 1965, I became the godfather of Peter and Anna Walker's son Philip - (I later put up the money for his education) - as well as of John and Ruth Doubleday's elder daughter Caroline. John Doubleday also appointed me as an executor of his Will (see illustration 77).

I was a heavy smoker in the 1960s. Smoking at the bridge table was commonplace. When I first joined the staff of the Kent Planning Department, I worked in an open-plan office. When Ash Wednesday came round, one of the girls in the office bet me that I couldn't give up smoking for Lent. I took the hint! I stopped smoking altogether. I have never smoked since. But smoking at the bridge table was still commonplace. I gave up playing bridge, as a result. But I did partner Peter Walker in one or two championship matches at Cheltenham, Richmond-on-Thames and Hastings. Harrison- Gray, the bridge correspondent of one of the national newspapers, was playing against us at Richmond-on-Thames. He saw my nervousness and kindly stopped my revoking when Peter and I were playing against him and his partner. In actual fact, Peter and I came out of this encounter rather well!

Today, there is a complete change in smoking etiquette. It is frowned on at the bridge table and, indeed, it is banned in the bridge rooms of all clubs. I have had no inhibitions against taking up the game again. First, I became a "relief" player in a skilled men's four in Kent. Peter Thomas, my old school Friend, was a regular member of this four. The four met once a week. The stakes were quite high at 25p. for 100 points.

Now, I play duplicate bridge weekly in two bridge clubs in Suffolk and the occasional game of social rubber bridge. I also play duplicate bridge during days at sea when I am on a cruise. On one particular cruise I had the great good fortune to play against (and occasionally partner) Tony Priday who had once captained the English national bridge team. I also play bridge regularly on my computer.

*

Visual arts have been an abiding interest. For many years, I was a Friend of the Royal Academy. I went to most of their exhibitions. I am also a Life Member of the Arts Fund. For several years I was a member of the local NADFAS branch in Aldeburgh. The Branch holds weekly lectures in the winter months and organises interesting excursions.

In the autumn of 2000, I had a fortnight's package holiday in the United States, largely devoted to visits to major art galleries.

Allied to the visual arts has been my interest in historic buildings. I am a Life Member of the National Trust and of the Ancient Monuments Society. For several years, I was also a member of English Heritage. In my travels abroad, particularly on the continent of Europe, I have been fortunate in visiting many ancient buildings and historic sites.

76. Antony Lucas (c.1980)

77. John Doubleday & Family (1979)

78. Bridge Tournament, Salisbury (Harare) – Peter Walker, J.J. Macpherson
G. Dessen, Author

# ENVOI

Dr. Johnson, who is credited with the invention of the genre of biography, said that biography must include "the beautiful and the base". That is equally true of autobiography. In the introduction to these memoirs, I said I would endeavour to tell the truth about my life. I hope I have succeeded. The text has no distortions and no embellishments. I have mentioned some faults, although I would prefer to forget them.

If what has emerged is a picture of a rather disgruntled and sexually repressed individual, may I modify this by saying that I have thoroughly enjoyed my life, with all its ups and downs? I have been particularly fortunate in that I have never suffered from depression, and have enjoyed relatively good physical health (despite four operations in the King Edward VII Hospital for Officers and one or two subsequent operations in the Ipswich Hospital).

I first penned these lines on board a container ship, the *Maersk Constantia,* travelling from Cape Town to Tilbury. Without the eighteen days of relative quiet and isolation, I doubt whether these memoirs would ever have been written. They have subsequently been up-dated and edited, but I have made no deletions or substantial alterations.

Before embarking at Cape Town on the *Maersk Constantia*, Heather and I had lunch on two or three occasions with two of her very old friends. They are South Africans of German/Austrian origin. Klaus Rolfes, the husband migrated to South Africa on the same ship as Heather in 1947. Although brought up on the continent, Klaus enjoyed British nationality. During a long conversation, he was heavily critical of the destruction of Leipzig by massive bombing raids towards the end of World War II. I thought he had a point.

Life is full of coincidences. The shipping line carrying us back to England was called *Safmarine,* originally the *South African Marine Corporation Limited.* It had been restructured and had changed hands several times since it was founded in 1946. At the outset, its first Managing Director was none other than Marshall of the Air Force Sir Arthur Harris, commonly known as *Bomber Harris.* It was he, together with Churchill, who was responsible for the blanket bombing of Leipzig. There is a further strange coincidence. When I was travelling on a *Swan Hellenic* cruise in 1992, I met the Hon. Nicholas Assheton and his wife Jackie. Jackie was the daughter of Bomber Harris. She said that when she went to the unveiling of the statue of her father in the City of London, the ceremony was somewhat marred by a number of protesters against the bombing of German cities towards the end of the war.

*

I will add a word or two about religion. I was brought up in the Anglican Christian faith. I was baptised (with water from the River Jordan) when I was an infant and I was confirmed (by the Bishop of Grantham in Lincoln Cathedral) aged about 12. At Dover College, daily attendance at a short service in the school chapel was compulsory. At Selwyn College, I regularly attended the college's Sunday services. Church attendance was a less regular feature during my working life, but I did read the Bible from cover to cover when I was camping in the bush in Northern Rhodesia

It was many years before I seriously questioned my Christian faith, I must have recited the Nicene Creed scores of times before owning to the fact that I did not believe that there was a God who was "the maker of heaven and earth and of all things visible and invisible". It seemed to me that there was conclusive scientific evidence to the contrary. There were other parts of the Nicene Creed, which is the bedrock of the Christian faith, which seemed to me to be apocryphal, to put it mildly.

Now, therefore, I classify myself as an agnostic. I attend church services only when there is a baptism, marriage or funeral of someone I know. Occasionally, however, I will attend choral evensong in a Cathedral, just for the sheer joy of the music and the pageantry, but I refrain from reciting the Creed or the Lord's Prayer.

I would add I believe death is total and final and that there is no such thing as "the resurrection of the dead". Great persons, of whom Christ is certainly one, as are Mozart and Shakespeare for example, certainly **live on**, and may live on for ever in the minds and actions of people, over the generations. But that is not **resurrection.** Memories of lesser mortals, of whom I am indubitably one, soon fade and die.

*

The Chaplain at Dover College once asked a few of the boys what they wished for most in life. Priggishly, my choice was *power*! I thought it would be marvellous to be a Member of Parliament, or a General, or the Governor of a Crown Colony. It was a stupid answer. And, as will have been seen, I didn't come anywhere near to any of these positions.

The Chaplain's own choice for the most rewarding thing in life was *friendship.* What a wise choice! I have certainly found that my friendships have meant more to me than anything else in life. I still have friends I made at school. I still have friends I made when I was in the army. I still have friends I made when I lived in Northern Rhodesia. I have made many more friends since then. Some, but not all of them, are mentioned in these memoirs. Some, sadly, are no longer with us – a concomitant of one's own increasing age. Some, sadly, I now see far less often than I would wish. But I hold in the highest esteem all those of my many friends still living. I salute them and say "thank you for your friendship".

# Index Nominum